STEPS OF

We live in an age where the image very often speaks louder than the word.

Geoffrey Stevenson has delighted thousands with his poignant and unforgettable mimes, highlighting God's unchanging truth and leaving us with impressions that stay in our minds long afterwards.

His wife Judith is one of the pioneers of dance in worship, and both she and Geoffrey have worked on missions of evangelism and renewal. Here for the first time are practical guidelines for dance and drama groups who wish to learn the techniques that will add new dimensions to their worship and outreach.

The book is divided into three parts, with the Mime and Dance sections beginning from either end, both illustrated with line drawings. In the middle is a section for both mime artists and dancers, to help them limber up and keep in shape.

Steps
of
Faith

A Practical Introduction to
Mime and Dance

GEOFFREY & JUDITH STEVENSON

KINGSWAY PUBLICATIONS
EASTBOURNE

ISBN 0 86065 275 0

Front cover photo (mime): Claire Oliver
Front cover photo (dance): John G. Stevenson

Illustrations (mime) by Vic Mitchell
Illustrations (dance) by Janet Lunt

Printed in Great Britain for
KINGSWAY PUBLICATIONS LTD
Lottbridge Drove, Eastbourne, E. Sussex BN23 6NT by
Richard Clay (The Chaucer Press) Ltd, Bungay, Suffolk.
Typeset by Nuprint Services Ltd, Harpenden, Herts.

Contents

DANCE

1. What Is Dance—Sacred, Secular or Silly?   8
2. The Challenge to Christians: Why We Should Dance 23
3. So Why Don't We Dance?   38
4. Worship   47
5. Try It, Try It, You Will See...   53
6. Keep Going—There Is More to Explore!   63
7. Congregational Dance   75
8. Dance Ministry   87
9. The Dance Group   101
   Appendix: Leading workshops   113

MAKE IT WORK   87

Bibliography   104

Acknowledgements   6
Foreword by Anne Watson   7
Introduction   9

MIME

1. What Is Mime?   14
2. Mime in the Church   19
3. Holding the Stage   32
4. Basic Mime   41
5. Character   49
6. Illusions   57
7. Creating Your Own Work   67
   Appendix: Notes on Performing Mime, and Two Pieces 72

Note

Please turn to the other end of the book for the Acknowledgements, Foreword by Anne Watson, and the Introduction.

Dance

1. *What Is Dance—Sacred, Secular or Silly?*

'Do you think the vicar wants us to conga up the aisles?'

'I can't imagine the congregation will approve of black leotards in front of the altar.'

'I don't think it would work, we don't have any music in church that would be suitable for ballet.'

Believe it or not, these are genuine comments that I have heard from members of congregations in different parts of the country. In spite of the growing interest in dance, many of us are so full of preconceived ideas about what dance is, and about what the attitude of the Christian and the church should be towards it, that we find it impossible to think that dance can play any part at all in our Christian lives.

Whatever preconceptions we have, however, there is no doubt that as far as secular society is concerned, dance is suddenly 'in'. At first I thought that because I was writing about dance, I was imagining the growing public interest—rather like buying a new car. Suddenly, every other car on the road is the same make as yours! But it isn't just me. Everything from leg warmers becoming a fashion accessory, to the popularity of television programmes such as *Fame,* indicates the new interest in dance.

It is more relevant than ever before to consider why we as Christians have so many different opinions about dance. Why is there so often so much opposition? Could dance eventually become an accepted part of the worship of every church? Could it become part of the life of every Christian?

As illustrated by the three comments at the beginning of this chapter, the word 'dance' itself can conjure up many different images in people's minds. Small wonder that there can be so much controversy at the idea of bringing 'dance' into the church. Thus it is obvious that before going any further it is necessary to discuss what dance actually is.

We have two small daughters, Elizabeth and Anna, aged five and three. They are the sort of children who are on the go all day, and then sleep like logs all night. I suppose having a mime artist for a father and a dancer for a mother must have something to do with it! Anyway, like

all small children they love to perform and they love to dance. It doesn't matter what the music is—be it a violin concerto or the latest in Christian rock. When they want to dance, they move! They skip and jump, spin and hop, roll on the floor, run round in circles and at last collapse in a dizzy heap, with much laughter and confusion.

Elizabeth and Anna are only imitating what they see, whether it is me in a church service, or ballet at the theatre, or disco on the television. The results are usually very funny and the hilarity is due to their amusement at themselves, as well as each other. Nevertheless, there is a wonderful spontaneity in their dancing and playing. They are completely unrestricted by self-consciousness and delightfully abandon themselves to the music. In doing so, they reveal their vulnerability and their complete trust in the audience, whether real or imaginary.

What is it that allows me to call their funny antics

'dance'? Their movements are uncoordinated and, to most people's eyes, very clumsy. Nevertheless, as I watch them I realize that they clarify my understanding of what dance is.

You see, dancing comes from the inside, not from the outside. No matter how simple or difficult the movement, there is, for each individual, a point at which a movement is not just moved, but is danced. Watching movement become dance is like watching a smouldering log burst into flames: suddenly there is life.

What before was only an indication suddenly becomes a reality. What before was only the body altering its position suddenly becomes the revelation of a human being as a whole person, body, mind and spirit. We can't define the soul of dance, any more than we can define the soul of man, and yet a human being without soul is not a man, and movement without soul is not dance.

It is important to understand that this definition of dance applies to all forms of movement, whether secular or sacred. Some Christians mistakenly assume that because of the Christian awareness of the presence of a soul, only in sacred dancing is there an expression of an inner life behind the outward form. In fact it is just as easy for a Christian as for a non-Christian to dance and not allow himself the freedom to lay bare his inner life so that it is on view to the whole world. In fact, if this is so, it cannot be called dance. Often in secular dance—and sadly, sometimes in sacred too—there are very good imitations, especially after years of hard physical training. But unless a dancer is willing to share himself freely, body, mind and spirit, with the audience, then however expert his movements, they cannot be called dance.

Animals don't dance. They may perform a series of movements that could be described as 'dance-like' (for example, some species of bird attract a mate with a dance-like ritual) but it is soul-less. Likewise, we may be able to execute a series of movements with superb ability and control, but it still may not be dance.

Secular dance

What about some of the more stylized forms of movement with which we are familiar? And what about recreational dancing? Is it possible to see that fine dividing line between movement and dance? Could it be that it is this that takes someone from the back of the chorus to stardom? After all, the chorus have all had the same opportunity to learn to execute with great skill a strict vocabulary of movement.

What makes a great dancer is the ability to learn with tremendous physical expertise a particular 'style' (ballet is the best example) and then to bring 'soul' to it. Nearly all of us will have seen, either on television or in person, the great ballerina, Dame Margot Fonteyn. If someone asked you what it was that made her dancing so extraordinarily beautiful, you would probably find it difficult to put into words, but you would know that you had seen someone dance with her whole being, almost giving herself personally to each member of the audience.

And yet classical ballet so often fails to live up to the potential seen in its greatest dancers. Its basic movements are stylized, rigidly defined, and rigorously formal. They can seem cold and inhuman, almost mechanical. Put these basic building blocks together and often all you get is an athletic and occasionally breath-taking display of movements that cause the observer to think 'Gosh, that must be difficult'. In fact, the judging of the technique of individual dancers becomes one of the most important parts of one's appreciation of the dance. Today's televised gymnasts may not aspire to such beauty in movement (although they're trying), but at least they are honest about their competitiveness.

The plot in a ballet, such as it is, advances laboriously, propelled by melodramatic mime gestures. The artifice often overwhelms the art, and sheer spectacle, or a prima ballerina on the bill, is the only way of appealing to a wide, paying audience.

This is a somewhat jaundiced viewpoint, and ballet enthusiasts will think it unfair in the extreme. Yet it was dissatisfactions like these, coupled with an ideal of dance as I have attempted to define it, that gave rise to an entirely new and different dance-form at the beginning of this century. Modern or contemporary dance looks and feels completely different. There were two great pioneers, Isadora Duncan and Ruth St Denis. They were both American and, finding little or no interest for their work in America, they came to Europe where they were received with open arms. Anyone who has seen old films of Isadora Duncan will know what I mean when I say that she moved as no one had ever seen anyone move before. Unrestricted by the accepted conventions of ballet, her dancing was a language in itself. It had a timeless quality to it that should never have earned the description 'modern'. If she is only remembered today because her costume on stage was sometimes rather scant, it is a great shame. Where ballet seems to try to defy gravity, Isadora *used* the floor or the ground. Whereas ballet seems to originate from the head, for Isadora dance originated from her soul. She said, 'I came to Europe to promote a renaissance of religion by means of the dance, to reveal the beauty and holiness of the human body by the openness of its movement.'

She eventually started a dance school in Paris, and from the spark of her vision others caught fire. The flame spread across Europe and eventually back to America. But if you attend a performance of modern dance today, it is likely that what you will see will have very little relationship to the dancing of the original pioneers. I have said that, for Isadora, dance originated from her soul; she believed that her soul was in her solar plexus. Of course, the inevitable has happened—a whole new style has been developed based on movement originating from the solar plexus, not from the soul! Some have gone further still, believing that the body is nothing but a moving thing in space, and that any overtones of meaning are completely coincidental. Surely dance can never be abstract, like modern painting or sculpture? Shapes and lines are shapes and lines. Dancers are people. They may *try* to become nothing more than objects in space, but they can only pretend, and the result is ugly.

Doris Humphrey, one of America's greatest modern dancers, says of this trend, 'Is it possible that this is a legitimate expression of the disillusionment of our time? Are people so bewildered and world-weary, so afraid of life and what it offers, that abstraction is a welcome retreat, behind which they need not think, feel or suffer? That, to me, is a very sad conclusion, but logical. A sick world will produce a sick art' (*Art of Making Dances* p.171).

Sometimes when I see very good contemporary dance I am amazed by the beauty of what I see, and by the range and depth of emotion that can be communicated. And yet other work, other performances, can leave me not just cold but almost repulsed. In this way dance reflects the prevailing philosophy of our time: it is on the one hand a striving to reveal the beauty and holiness of man in a way that dance has never before been allowed to (as painting and sculpture have) and, on the other hand, it is man screaming out his rejection of God and himself and his environment, and showing himself to be little more than a civilized animal.

Less easy to analyse is the ethnic dance of cultures other than our own. Ethnic dance is an umbrella term, it seems, for all kinds of traditional dancing indigenous to countries and cultures other than our own. It often strikes us with its beauty, its freshness, and its integrity, for it can seem to us marvellously unpolluted by the contradictions and tensions apparent in our own traditions of ballet and contemporary dance.

Its origins may be folk dancing or religious ritual, but the dance has in many places been refined and developed to produce performances of great beauty and majesty, with fantastic costumes and masks of brilliant colours and striking appearance. Usually these are an integral part of the handed-down tradition. The actual dance movements may be strictly defined, with a limited vocabulary. Nevertheless, the dancers themselves dance with a passion borne of a love of their country and its past, and we as the audience are transported to a different time and place. Such is the power of the art of dance.

But what about all the popular forms of dance, such as folk dancing, ballroom and disco? These are what most people do, albeit often in their own fashion. Are they conscious of a union of body, mind, soul and spirit? Are they aware of combining soul with style? Yes, I think that all these things apply to recreational dance.

Ballroom and folk dancing are similar in that they require a certain co-ordination to master basic steps which are then combined and strung together in patterns limited only by the stamina and memory of the dancers. A certain sense of style comes in, to adopt the right carriage, postures, bearing, and even attitude. Finally, there is the ability to dance *with* another, or others.

We must never forget the powerful appeal of simple dance steps, nor may we ignore the fact that these types of dance are so widely accepted in our culture.

Folk dance, such as Scottish country dancing, has obviously lost out over the years to other forms of recreation, most notably television. Few, however, given the chance, can resist or condemn the wholesome enjoyment offered by a lively reel. As a group activity bringing people together with laughter, fun and relaxation (if you know the steps!), folk dancing is hard to beat. And we shall see the relevance of Israeli dancing to our Christian life together a little further on in the book.

Disco dancing is another story. Under this title comes a whole variety of movement, some of which I see as a stunning and highly expressive art form. Although it is undoubtedly infused with the sexual suggestiveness of our society today, I cannot condemn it out of hand. But I would advise approaching it with caution and discernment.

A lot of what passes for dancing at rock concerts and 'heavy' discos, however, is unworthy of the name. Head-banging is the common term for it at the time of writing, which is a more or less complete description of the activity. Some will disagree, but there can be no union of body, mind and spirit when the body is uncontrolled, the mind absent and the spirit wrapped up in total isolation from everyone and everything except the never-ending heavy beat.

A question I am very often asked is, should Christians go to a disco? Lest we stick our heads in the sand yet again in an attempt to remain unsullied by the world, let's ask ourselves who is going to reach out and draw alongside the punks and head-bangers to share the *love* and good news of Christ? Not the local vicar and his deacons. Let's not be so pig-headed as to imagine that just because a Christian is only sixteen years old and has an exuberance that we lack, he or she could not be a very strong and powerful witness for the Lord. If you want to go to a disco, go as Christ sent his disciples, in twos or more, and enjoy yourself. But remember that the Lord will show himself in who you are and what you do, and that he might want to use what *you* say to speak to others about himself.

Sacred dance

Ballet is as far from disco as Haydn is from Heavy Metal, and yet it is still called dance. The range in sacred dancing is scarcely less. I am describing it and analysing it separately because it is different from secular dance.

Sacred dance is set apart, not by its style or its vocabulary of movement, but by the desire of the participant to see glory and praise given, not to themselves, nor to the art of dance, but to God. It is set apart also because the two essential elements of dance, a unity of body, mind and spirit and a freedom to express that unity, are two of the essential elements of our lives as re-born Christians.

Sacred dancing is, therefore, so much more than secular dancing because when the freedom that it requires is God-given, and when the unity of body, mind and spirit is part of the redemptive process of God working in one of his children, then the dancing becomes one of the most beautiful things we will see this side of heaven.

Recently I watched a small group of women of all ages dancing for God. It *was* dancing, even though looked at objectively through the eyes of a trained dancer, they were uncoordinated and clumsy. Not only were they dancing, but there was great beauty in what they were doing. Their freedom was *real* freedom, freedom that comes only when we become slaves of God. And as they expressed outwardly parts of their personalities that are normally hidden, they made themselves vulnerable. As they expressed physically the mental, emotional and spiritual aspects of their natures, those of us watching saw not the 'old man', but a wonderful reflection of Jesus, and in their willingness to be vulnerable we saw the love of God when he made *himself* vulnerable in giving his only Son for us. Small wonder it was beautiful.

I have seen Christians discover the wonder of sacred dancing many times, whether they are dancing them-

selves, or watching others minister in dance. Even if I am
only asking them to raise their arms in worship, suddenly,
instead of just mechanically imitating me, I see real freedom and vulnerability expressed in that simple gesture.

Sacred dance can as easily be a mixture of all the other
forms, as it can be pure ballet, folk or contemporary.
When led by the Spirit it can be a most perfect response of
man to his Creator and Redeemer. It can also be nothing
more than a series of ugly and meaningless movements,
with little effect other than to give the visitors to the
church something to write home about!

In the summer of 1974 'Shekinah' visited York. They were a group of singers, dancers and musicians touring the country, inspiring others to worship and praise the Lord. Two dancers, a singer, a musician and a poet stayed in our home. They were the most exciting people I had ever met, because I had never been with a group of people before who were so openly in love with Jesus, *and* committed to one another.

The service of praise that they led in York Minster was fantastic. Quite simply, they directed the gaze of all of us there to Jesus, and they gave us a new vision of God— which is what leading worship is all about. It was the first time I had ever seen sacred dance. I think there were eight dancers, six girls and two men. Their costumes were the costumes of people who were celebrating, people who knew they were the children of a King. Dresses in reds, golds, purples and greens, ribbons flowing from their hair and wrists, they danced to the songs that were sung—perhaps to some music that was purely instrumental, I don't remember. Some of their dances were truly folk dances, and although no one else was able to join in, just watching them seemed to strengthen the commitment of the Christians in York to one another. Some of their dances were more balletic in style. They offered themselves, body, mind and spirit, in a sacrifice of praise to God. The result was that our eyes and minds were drawn away from them, and directed up to God and to God only. Perhaps this is why I don't remember the details very well. I just remember being taken up into the heavenly places, and seeing God as I had never seen him before. Truly, God is seen in the praises of his people.

It is all too easy for us to view such worship services with apprehension. We label such freedom as being out of control and mindless emotionalism. But we react from deep within our own culture, and in particular our stiff upper English lip! Freedom is threatening so we lash out with our ever-ready tongues in defence of all that we wish to keep hidden.

There are many different forms of sacred dance because the Holy Spirit speaks to and inspires different cultures, congregations and individuals in a variety of ways. It is impossible to describe all the dance that has ever taken place in the history of the Christian church. I intend merely to pick out a few examples to give you some idea of what you are missing!

At the top of the list (in terms of numbers participating) comes all the movement that is so much part of Third World Pentecostalism. Not only do these people respond to God with their whole being—body, mind and spirit— but their way of passing on the values of the past is through music and dance.

The Chilean Pentecostal movement describes its own beginnings in 1904, a breakaway from the missionary-dominated Methodist Church, as follows: 'The brethren were possessed by dancing and spiritual visions, they spoke in tongues of angels, prophesying about the great spiritual revival. The Holy Spirit seized them in the streets. The authorities took them into the prisons as criminals, but the brethren danced in the prisons, speaking in tongues and prophesying to these officials.'

What an amazing picture of revival. It reminds me in so many respects of the birth of the church in Acts 2. If you visited a Pentecostal church in Chile today, you would find that the people still dance. They are often circular-based dances, reminiscent of their Indian ancestry. Those who don't join in stand at the sides and clap reverently. At the end, the whole congregation fall on their knees to thank God for the dance he has given them. These people respond to God with their whole beings, and their way of passing on the values of the past is through music and dance.

Because the Chileans (and the blacks in America)

have a long history of dance, it is an ability they inherit, it seems, in the same way that all Welshmen sing! The Holy Spirit comes and inspires this natural ability, and dance becomes a beautifully controlled and integral part of the Pentecostal service.

In the West, dancing has often been and sometimes still is part of the worship of the established churches, both Roman Catholic and Anglican. It seems that almost always the inspiration is found in the Eucharist or the daily office. Also, more often than not, the dance ties in with the processional or recessional hymn, whether it is performed by a special group, or by the congregation. This is hardly surprising, of course, because the church members are familiar with movement at the beginning and at the end of the service and therefore it is easier to take this just one step further.

What is most exciting is that liturgical dance in the established churches is on the increase. For example, in 1967 at the Metropolitan Cathedral in Liverpool, the opening service of dedication was followed by an event of music, dance and drama. Many of the dancers were highly trained, and came from many different countries. The style of the dancing was more modern than balletic, and simply expressed the prayers of the mass.

The Anglican cathedrals have not missed out either. In Ripon Cathedral in 1972, a group of young people, under the direction of the Reverend Maxwell Fergus, danced the gloria, the offertory and the post-communion during a service to celebrate the thirteenth-century celebrations.

In fact, I was in Ripon Cathedral only a few weeks ago watching dance. This time the dancers were a well-known Christian dance company called 'Springs'. They performed a series of short pieces, some comical, some utterly beautiful, using a wide range of music and style. This small company of four girls serve the Lord by travelling around the country, taking part in festivals and missions and leading workshops.

Another well-known and full-time Christian dance company is the Sacred Dance Group. The Lord has given this group a most wonderful ministry of using dance to reach out and touch people's lives with the love of Jesus. Perhaps this is because they so clearly see that the gift of dance that the Lord has given them is only a means to an end, and not an end in itself.

A lot of the sacred dance described here has been that seen publicly, executed by full-time or semi-professional dancers. As seen in South American Pentecostalism, however, dance is relevant to every individual; it is a part of our humanity that God has given us to express ourselves, and through which we can give joy to him.

Dance is a means whereby you and I might draw closer to Jesus. It is a means whereby Jesus might reach down and minister to us. It is a means whereby we might reach up and minister to Jesus, and finally it is a means whereby the body of Christ and his kingdom might be seen by the outside world.

2. The Challenge to Christians: Why We Should Dance

Dance builds up God's people and extends the kingdom. 'You are not going to suggest, are you, that we should *all* dance?'

No, I am not suggesting that we should all dance all of the time, but I do think that every Christian should have such a complete comprehension of himself as a created, unified being, that the idea of using his body in his relationship with God should be completely natural.

'But why is this so important? Aren't we all right as we are?'

No, I really don't think that most of us are OK. There is a desperate hunger in the world to know Jesus, and among his people to know him better. The Lord is pouring out his Spirit in great power, but there is a danger that some of us are not ready to be the vessels God wants to receive that power, and to pass it on to the world. God is saying to us, 'Prepare the way of the Lord, make yourselves ready to do my work in the days to come.' We stand before our Lord, and we ask him to use us as his servants in the days ahead. Yet we sense that we are still working at a fraction of the power that is available to us.

I believe that this is because we have a misunderstanding of ourselves as redeemed, whole, complete beings. We are aware of the necessity for the salvation of the mind and spirit, but we ignore the body. We ignore the physical. We ignore the fact that God has created us as moving, seeing, hearing, feeling beings.

If we are willing to use movement and dance in our own personal times with God, as well as with others in large and small groups, God will work in us and upon us. He will bring us so much closer to becoming that whole person that he longs to see.

I have seen people 'come alive' through dance many, many times. For example, some years ago a minister from Northern Ireland, whose denomination I can't remember, visited our church. He joined us for a week of meetings on renewal and chose to come to the seminars on dance. There is no doubt that that in itself required a certain degree of humility, as all the other men chose subjects such as evangelism or ministry or music. At the end of the week that man's testimony was that God using dance had completely changed his life. In his willingness to give himself wholly to God, body, mind and spirit, God was able to heal hurts and bitternesses. The Lord was also able to fill this man's life so full of his power that I sometimes still hear about the way he is being used afresh by God in

Northern Ireland—full of God's Spirit and his power.

Why is it that God can use dance? Why is it that more and more people across Britain and America are dancing before the Lord in a fresh response to the pouring out of his Spirit? Why should there be any real need for you or me to express what we feel on the outside, as well as on the inside? We say to ourselves, 'It's what I feel on the inside that counts. I can worship the Lord quite well enough standing up with my hands by my sides. I can be just as repentant sitting as I can kneeling. I don't need to move my lips to pray.' Can we? I don't believe it is enough. But why is it that we have such an unbalanced view of ourselves, and one that makes the idea of dance so difficult? What should our attitude be? What does the Bible teach us?

To be honest, most of us find ourselves in a position of complete uncertainty as to how to regard our bodies. Some of us are confused because on the one hand we are taught to 'pummel our body and subdue it', and yet we are aware that constantly denying ourselves sleep, for example, can result in a life that is no use whatsoever to the Lord.

This dilemma has increased over the past ten years, because of the sudden explosion of interest in the Western world in physical health and well-being. As you see your next-door neighbour set off for a 2-mile jog every morning before work, you may think to yourself, 'He is concerned with preservation of his body, but I know that it is preservation of the soul that is most important.' As I chat with the other mothers at play-group about needing to lose weight, I think to myself, 'Vanity, vanity, and to be vain is a sin, and anyway, my husband loves the inside me, not the outside me.' As my mother spots an advertisement in a women's magazine telling her that if she uses a certain skin lotion she will find the secret of eternal youth, she thinks to herself, 'I don't want eternal youth, I have eternal life.' When we go for lunch to a new young couple in the church who are interested in health foods, we think to ourselves, 'Of course, we are so busy with our Christian lives, we don't have time for thinking about food.'

What is the result? A church of overweight, dowdy women and exhausted, shabby men, all smiling hard because they are sure it's more spiritual to have had only six hours sleep instead of seven.

Of course I am exaggerating. There are times in all our lives, as in the life of the apostle Paul, when our bodies receive mistreatment, neglect and real physical suffering. In such a condition many a Christian seems to radiate the love of Jesus, his compassion, his holiness and his humility.

Our problem is that we try to make asceticism and bodily denial a condition for spirituality, and it ends up being a substitute for a pure heart (see Col 2:20–23).

What does the Bible say about our humanity? How did Jesus regard himself as a physical as well as a spiritual being? In Genesis 1 we read how God created us. We read that everything he made was good and pleasing to him. As we continue on through the Old Testament it soon becomes clear to us that God was just as much concerned for the material needs of his people as he was for their spiritual needs. Not only did he provide for them, but he gave them simple directions regarding cleanliness and health. The Jews didn't need scientific proof as to whether these laws were beneficial to their lives or not. They accepted that God, their Creator, would know best how their bodies needed to be taken care of.

Jesus himself teaches that we should ask God to provide for our physical needs: 'Give us today our daily bread.' Sadly, most of us in the Western world don't really trust God enough to be certain that he will supply our daily bread. Either we are so well provided for that the idea never crosses our minds, or we believe that it isn't spiritual to be concerned about the needs of the flesh. The reason that we have this unbalanced view of what is spiritual and what isn't, is because of an unbalanced view of ourselves as human beings.

From the Hebrew perspective human beings do not have bodies, they *are* bodies. They do not have souls, they *are* souls. There is no rigid distinction between the physical and the spiritual because body and soul are so intimately united that dichotomy is impossible. The Jew regarded his body as the outward form of his soul. The Old Testament speaks of the whole human being not as a discarnate spirit, but as a spiritual corporeal entity. The New Testament understanding is the same. Read the writings of Paul with this Hebrew perspective in mind. When Paul writes of 'the body' he means the whole human being: 'Do you not know that your body is a temple of the Holy Spirit, who is in you, whom you have received from God? You are not your own; you were bought at a price. Therefore honour God with your body' (1 Cor 6:19, NIV). 'The body is...for the Lord, and the Lord for the body' (1 Cor 6:13, NIV).

Unfortunately as soon as I exhort a group of Christian women to take more care of their bodies, I am equated with the glossy magazine that exhorts its readers to think of nothing *but* the body. So I explain that whereas the glossy magazine appeals to us all to fit into the same mould, as God's children *every* different mould is a wonderful creation. When Jesus went to the cross and paid for us the highest price ever paid, the 'us' that he bought was not just mind and spirit, but the whole being, body, mind and spirit. Surely, in the light of this knowledge, we should be able to walk with our heads held high, and a bounce in our step.

Finally, God set his seal on our humanity in the incarnation of his Son. When the New Testament speaks of the resurrection, and of the after-life, it is speaking of each person in his or her wholeness, a unified and healed personality. To put it more simply, you are what you are because of what you stand up in. When we join Christ in heaven, the you who is you and the me who is me will be perfected and whole, but it will still be you and me! Our bodies will be renewed (hallelujah!) but not so that they no longer fit with us as individuals.

So, you say to yourself, maybe I haven't had a proper understanding of the holiness of the body, maybe I haven't seen myself as a unified being of body and soul. But what has all this to do with dance?

Consider what is perhaps the strongest image the Bible gives us of salvation: the image of Christ taking in his body our twisted, sinful and shattered lives, and making them whole and perfect through that death on the cross. A human life without Christ suffers the consequences of sin. That human life, instead of being the whole and beautiful piece of creation that God meant it to be, is instead cracked and broken, with many of its parts warped or unused. We know that if Christ came into that life, he would begin to heal and to mend, to bind up and make whole.

More than any other human activity, dance can reflect that transition from brokenness to wholeness. Also, because dance requires the participant to be unified in body and spirit, it can be the very means whereby God actually brings about the healing of that brokenness.

As you read this your reaction may be one of mistrust and disbelief, especially if your experience of liturgical dance is not of something that has brought about harmony and peace, but instead just the opposite. As I write this, I am on holiday in Scotland with a family who are in a leadership position in a church near London. We have spent time over the past couple of days talking about this church's dance group. Anna confessed to me today that one of the reasons she would quite happily remain in north Scotland for ever is her apprehension concerning the problems surrounding this dance group at home.

My advice to her is to persevere. The group is still very new, and those involved are only just beginning to learn about movement and dance. In the words of our wise friend David Smith, sometimes you have to be 'upset' before you can get 'reset'. The first year may be fraught with difficulties while individuals learn to deal with things inside themselves that the Holy Spirit has brought to the surface through the dance. If the members are willing to persevere, Anna will find that 'upsets will become reset', and the members will grow with the Lord as never before.

I think that we Christians can be very guilty of ignoring the experience and professional advice that the world has to offer in some areas. In particular, our approach to counselling can be shameful. We can probably all think of someone in our fellowship who is 'known as having problems'. If we are not careful, the help that we give to that person is so 'airy' that it is totally useless. What I am getting at is that the world of psychotherapy has long understood that part of the work of putting back together a shattered and broken life is to help that person identify with their body. We should have so much more to offer as Christians. If we were also to grasp this, not only could we teach people to relate to their bodies, but, more importantly, we could teach people to use their bodies in their relationship with God and so receive his healing power into their lives. My longing is for dance to become such a natural part of our lives, both personal and corporate, that God's redemptive process, working in the lives of each of us, might amaze the world.

Of course, if dance *is* to have any relevance in our lives, it must 'amaze the world'. When we consider any aspect of our corporate lives as Christians we must ask the question, 'Does it build up the body of Christ, and does it extend his kingdom?' Dance not only upbuilds and strengthens the members of the church, but it also, in a very real and exciting way, shows the world that we are alive!

It shows the world that we are alive because we as individuals are involved in it, our lives are changed, and the people among whom we live see that God is at work in us. Dance teaches us the freedom to be ourselves. This results in a greater openness and ability to communicate God's love to our neighbours and friends. Jesus told us to go into the world and share the good news. If at the moment you or I find this difficult, it may well be that dance could lead us into a new freedom to be a witness for Christ.

The gospel is also spread inside the church, when dance is used as part of a service. We found in York that over and over again it would be the dance during a service that would touch the heart of a non-Christian visitor. God is revealed to the world through his people. When one of his children is caught up in worship to him in dance, the outsider sees the most wonderful reflection of a creator— redeemer God. A creator God, because when dancing, the beauty of each human being is seen as his wonderful creation. A redeemer God, because dance reflects and enhances the redemptive process of salvation. Through dance the invisible shows forth as well as the visible. Joy and sorrow, pain and grief, peace and freedom, hope and fulfilment are all portrayed by a dancer.

We live in a world so desperately in need of God's love and compassion. If God can express himself so powerfully through dance, surely we reject it at our peril. If you and I are offered a deeper and more living relationship with God through making dance a natural part of our lives, then we should take those steps of faith without any hesitation. If I didn't believe that dance is a means where-by we as Christians might grow closer to Jesus, and a means whereby others might be brought into his kingdom, then I should set it aside and have nothing more to do with it. The time is too short for tinkering with new fads that we think just might be useful to our Christian lives.

Dance is biblical

In the light of all that I have discussed in the first part of this chapter, it is not difficult to understand how dance was so much a part of the life of God's people in the Old Testament.

When the Israelites worshipped, they danced, whether it was a spontaneous response to God's goodness in giving them victory over their enemies, or whether it was a planned part of an annual festival. The actual scriptural references are many, and we mustn't assume that if it isn't mentioned that it wasn't happening. In fact, when we see the words 'to make merry, to rejoice' and sometimes even 'to prophesy', we can be sure that dancing was taking place during the beating of batons, the twanging of strings and the infectious rhythm of hard drums, castanets and cymbals.

It is not necessary here to look at every explicit reference to dance in the Old Testament, although I would encourage you to do so if you know that the Lord is leading you into a dance ministry. Apart from the obvious joy of doing this for its own sake, God's people in the Old Testament danced for the same reasons that we do today, and much can be learnt from a thorough study. Also, when meeting the objections of anyone who is unsure about dance for a Christian, it is obviously necessary to show that it is utterly scriptural.

1 Samuel 18:6–7 gives us a wonderful picture of spontaneous celebration, as the women of Israel went out to meet their victorious army. The song they sang was in praise of God's great battle warriors, David and Saul:

> When the men were returning home after David had killed the Philistine, the women came out from all the towns of Israel to meet King Saul with singing and dancing, with joyful songs and with tambourines and lutes. As they danced, they sang (NIV).

I wish I could have been there! It must have been an amazing sight. The people of Israel were so aware of God's hand upon them. They were aware that when there was victory it meant that God was pleased with them, and so the response to the victory was one of worship. They praised David and Saul, but they knew that it is the Lord who gives and the Lord who takes away.

Also, it was through song and dance that the Jewish people memorized and passed on their history. We see how this has happened in 1 Samuel 21:11, as the servants of the King of Gath speak to King David. 'Isn't this David, the king of the land? Isn't he the one they sing about in their dances?'

It is also interesting to note how often dancing is mentioned as the opposite of mourning. As I read the Old Testament, I realize how much 'mourning and weeping' must have been part of the life of the Israelites. As far as their material needs were concerned, there were years of plenty, but there were also barren years when they had to trust God day by day to provide them with food and shelter. So often they turned away from God, and each time he drew them back to himself and forgave them when they repented. Then there was great rejoicing at God's goodness to them, and at such times their joy was so great that only through dancing could they give full expression to their emotions.

In Ecclesiastes 3:4 we read there is 'a time to weep and a time to laugh, a time to mourn and a time to dance' (NIV). God doesn't change, and this statement is as true for us today as it was when it was written. As we grow in the Lord we learn to enter into his sufferings in order that we can also enter into his victory. Before I knew the Lord, I never wept or mourned as I have done since I became a Christian. But at the same time I never knew the breathtaking joy that there is when he takes us up into the heavenly places. I believe we shall all dance in heaven, because it is the most natural way of expressing wholeness and joy that God has given us.

I have a friend whose baby died in her cot when she was three months old. There followed many, many months of deep, deep grieving. But the Lord's promise is that he will turn our mourning into dancing. Six months after the death of the baby, I spent one very wonderful day with this friend. Her testimony is that after the valley, God had truly lifted her into the mountain tops. She now has a joy and a peace far greater than anything she had previously known. She seems to be literally walking on air—dancing for her Lord. She says with the Psalmist, 'You turned my wailing into dancing; you removed my sackcloth and clothed me with joy' (Ps 30:11–13, NIV).

Perhaps the best-known reference to dancing in Scripture is that of King David before the advancing Ark (see 2 Sam 6 and 1 Chron 15). Two things should be noted here. The first is that just because we don't read of any other kings who dance, we should not assume that David was the only one. The reason that the incident is particularly noted is because of Michal's (David's wife) reaction to it. In fact, it was part of the duty of the king to take the leading priestly role in the festival, and dance wearing the ephod.

Secondly, David's answer to Michal when she accuses him of 'disrobing in the sight of the slave girls as any vulgar fellow would!' was, 'I will celebrate before the Lord. I will become even more undignified than this.' Quite a challenge to us, I think, to ask ourselves if we are ready to sacrifice everything, even our dignity, to make a 'sacrifice of praise' to the Lord.

Dance was also a means of communication. Some dancers in particular were called evangelists and the 'society of prophets' sang and danced God's message to his people. In Psalm 68 we read of a procession where the 'good news' of God's greatness is proclaimed by the prophets and then taken and passed on to the whole assembly:

> In front are the singers, after them the musicians; with them are the maidens playing tambourines. Praise God in the great congregation; praise the Lord in the assembly of Israel (vv. 25–26, NIV).

The Jews worshipped and praised God with dance. We see that dance was a natural expression for each individual, in particular as a response of thanksgiving to God as he forgave sins and as he saved individuals and the nation from affliction. We see that dance played a major role in annual festivals and in the liturgy.

Before writing this, I read an essay by J. H. Eaton called 'Dancing in the Old Testament', which opened up for me a whole new understanding of how dance could and perhaps should be an integral part of the worship of a God-fearing people. However, I think I ought to mention Professor Eaton's suggestion that the dance itself, or indeed, the music that accompanied it, contained an 'uncanny power' that could 'control spirits good or bad'. It is possible that you will also come across those who may use this reason for objecting to the use of dance in the church today.

The answer to such an objection is that when the Holy Spirit works in and through God's servants, it is characterized by the individual being in full control, rather than the manifestation controlling the individual (see 1 Cor 14:32–33). It is entirely wrong to conclude that when Hebrew priests and priestesses gave themselves in worship to God, that dancing was used to whip up the worshippers to exhilaration and ecstasy. Rather, it was a natural expression of love and joy before a great and mighty God.

By contrast, the New Testament is virtually silent on dance, as it is on so many aspects of the life of the early Christians. In the Gospels Jesus refers to dancing twice—in the parables of the prodigal son and the children in the market-place. The other (unfortunate) exception is the dancing of Salome. There is no doubt, however, that God's chosen people, those chosen by him to receive his Son into the world, were a dancing people.

The fact that when Jesus was born the Jews were under Roman oppression meant that dance probably became more important to them rather than less. Indeed, there are modern examples that show that to a people who are culturally oppressed, exuberant worship becomes more important than ever. W. J. Hollenweger gives two examples of this:

The black people who were shipped to the USA had lost their own tradition, their language and their culture, but they had not lost their songs and their dances.

And of the Pentecostal movement in Chile:

As in the case of the Negroes, their culture, language and religion have been destroyed, but not their dances and their music. It [the dance] is a vital form of expression for a people who are forced to talk the language of those who have persecuted and almost wiped them out.

We have no proof that Jesus danced, although it should be noted that it is even more difficult to prove he did *not* dance. In the processions going up to Jerusalem for the major festivals, would he not have danced with everyone else? At the wedding in Cana, would he not have joined in the rejoicing? At such weddings it was only the old and infirm who were allowed to sit out.

I am not trying to argue that Jesus danced in order to persuade you that you must too. All I am suggesting is that we allow the picture we have of Jesus' earthly life and ministry to be enlarged to include the dance that was part of his culture and the everyday life of his people.

Ask yourself, have we come so far in our own culture, and are we going in the right direction?

In Revelation 19 we read:

Let us rejoice and exult and give him the glory, for the marriage of the Lamb has come, and his Bride has made herself ready; it was granted her to be clothed with fine linen, bright and pure (RSV).

Do you feel like a bride preparing herself for a marriage? When you join with other Christians, do you sense that excitement and expectancy that a family has as its members array themselves to go to a wedding? When the marriage of the Lamb comes, will we be ready to be the bride? I was recently reminded that I had better learn to sing now, because I would be doing plenty of it in heaven. Perhaps we ought to be learning to dance now, in order to dance as the bride at the marriage feast. I don't think it is a coincidence that when we dance outside our church during the summer, tourists come up and ask if there is going to be a wedding! 'Yes,' we answer, 'come into the service with us, and find out about it!'

3. *So Why Don't We Dance?*

'To be honest,' said my brother David, 'even if we suggested to the elders that perhaps just the children put together a simple dance for the Sunday morning service, I don't think they would agree.' David and his wife have recently moved to Scotland, where they have committed themselves to a church where there *are* Christians, and where the gospel *is* preached, but where there is a great resistance to any fresh approach to worship. 'Why is it that some people are so against any form of physical expression?' David continued. 'They would never dream of raising their arms in worship, let alone giving a fellow Christian an occasional hug!'

'Have you asked them why they are so resistant to the idea?' I asked.

'Yes,' said David, 'I did ask one man. He kept his hands very firmly clasped behind his back as he told me that it is unseemly and unspiritual to have any regard for the flesh, and that bodily expression is, at best, superficial! And then he added as an afterthought that such things are just not British.'

For the duration of its history, the church in Great Britain has, on the whole, been opposed to dance. But why such opposition when dance was so much a part of the life and times of Jesus? Why such opposition when it can express so wonderfully the mystery of our salvation? Why such opposition when community dancing is such a natural way of coming together with people you love?

If the church has been opposed, has dance ever actually taken place in the buildings of the established denominations, or is the opposition purely hypothetical? It *is* true that no mention of dance is made in documents prior to the fourth century, but it is hardly surprising when you consider that the Christian church was often forced to go underground, meeting in homes. They had the same problem that I have when a prayer group meets in my own sitting-room: there isn't enough space to dance!

Once the church began to have its own buildings, dancing reappeared. An anonymous homily of the fourth century contains the exhortation, 'If you will, let us celebrate in his honour our accustomed dances.' Throughout the Middle Ages, Easter, Christmas and other feast days were the occasion for dancing in cathedrals, collegiate churches and parish churches.

So why did the church leaders feel so strongly the need to expel dancing of all kinds from church buildings? The reason was that although much of it was indicative of true worship, and was done in that spirit, and with great reverence, there was also much that was a desecration. For example at St Edward's, Sarum, in England, we find reference to maypole dancing in the nave in 1490. Not worship, but rather a form of jollification, which related more to a pagan past. I have heard folk jokingly recall that one reason why the bishops tried to bring an end to dancing was that it was because of this that John the Baptist lost his head!

Still, what the bishops and the church councils called 'desecration' and 'fleshly' some people might only have described as 'having a good time'. And after all, what is wrong with joy and celebration in the house of God? Why were the thinkers of the first centuries after Christ so wary of regarding the physical part of each human being with as much respect as the mental or the spiritual?

The fault lies at the door of the philosopher and thinker Plato. His way of explaining the make-up of every individual was tremendously influential, and has become known as 'Platonic dualism'. Plato understood human beings to be a union of soul and body, but he regarded the former as being far superior to the latter. In fact he despised the body for the way it restricted the soul. It was a prison, from which the only way of escape was death. Sounds familiar, doesn't it! Plato may have lived 2,400 years ago, but as far as I can see many of us still think in the same way.

Perhaps it was natural that as the early church began to grow, it sought to come to terms with the thought world of the Greek-Roman culture. Church leaders in the early centuries were mostly Roman citizens by upbringing and outlook. Sadly, as they turned their backs on the immoral society confronting them, where there were gross sexual perversion and heresies that encouraged sexual licence, they lost much of their respect for the physical body.

As the centuries passed, other philosophies reinforced such attitudes. 'Cartesian dualism' preached that the mind is far superior to all matter. The philosopher, Descartes, said 'I think, therefore I am'. He saw the body as being in existence due only to the power of the mind, devaluing the body and its language completely. So from its earliest beginnings the Christian church found itself bowing to the opinions of the thinkers in the world around it, and coming to the conclusion that any form of dance in church buildings was wrong.

Well, you say to yourself, there must be more to it than this. Surely my church isn't still under the influence of the thinking of Plato or Descartes? After all, the denomination to which I belong is only a hundred years old. What happened at the Reformation?

Unfortunately, the events of the Reformation only helped to confirm every true Englishman in the belief that in order to be truly godly, the desires and expressions of the body must be suppressed. The Lion Handbook entitled *The History of Christianity* says of Protestantism: 'Reformed men wanted worship to be as simple and as Scriptural as possible. It can be argued that features in worship not prescribed in Scripture, should be seen as forbidden.' In order to purify worship of all the so-called meaningless ritual that the reformers found in Roman Catholicism, many Protestants began to teach that anything other than the most basic form of church services was of the devil.

As far as the reformers were concerned, dance was definitely out. Not only was it forbidden in church, it was even scorned as a pleasurable pastime. The puritanical view of life was suspicious of *all* pleasure, relating pleasure to self-indulgence, and therefore seeing it as sinful.

It is almost as if some people believe that our British reserve is a gift from God, and must be preserved at all costs. In fact, most of us are influenced far more by traditions and events of the past than we realize. We think that because a certain attitude is prevalent in our church, it must be biblical and God's will. Jesus was right when he said we are like sheep. We blindly follow the opinions of the majority, without stopping to think why we go this way or that.

That dear Scotsman who expressed to my brother his very low opinion of any bodily expression, has probably been influenced far more by his Victorian grandparents than he realizes. My father describes himself as being brought up 'in the Victorian manner'. He therefore unconsciously grew up to believe that 'to be respectable' should be high on the list of achievements. To be respectable is to conform to a long list of acceptable modes of behaviour, and self-expression is not on the list.

The result is that when you or I suggest to our church or fellowship that our worship could be enhanced by using some sort of movement, we come up against attitudes that have a huge weight of history behind them. David Watson said in his book *God's Freedom Fighters:* 'For some time in evangelical circles, we have talked about a "worldly" Christian as one who smokes, drinks, dances and gambles and so on; and a non-worldly spiritual Christian as one who doesn't smoke, and doesn't drink and doesn't dance and doesn't gamble.' It is part of the traditional teaching of many a denomination, including the evangelicals, as David Watson says, to regard popular dancing as one of the worldly pursuits that should be avoided at all costs— the very idea of bringing it into church or indeed into any area of one's life, is completely abhorrent.

Although there are, of course, some areas that the Christian should completely avoid, we too easily fall into the trap of entirely avoiding some things that the Lord has in fact given us to enrich our lives. Paul says in the first three verses of 1 Timothy 4 that an excessively negative attitude to the world (you mustn't do these things, you mustn't do those things) could be a doctrine of demons! And in verse 4 and 5: 'For everything God created is good, and nothing is to be rejected if it is received with thanksgiving, because it is consecrated by the word of God and prayer' (NIV).

I believe that God wants us to redeem dance from the way that Satan uses it in the world, and make it once more a wholesome and very beautiful part of our relationship with him.

Apart from the objections to dance that arise from outside influences, there are what I call personal objections, which I suspect are niggling away at the back of someone's mind when they say something like, 'I'm not really sure why I object to dance, it just doesn't seem right, that's all'. In fact, I would have made almost exactly the same comment myself fifteen years ago.

Before I became a Christian, I enjoyed dancing as much as anyone. I went to barn dances in the country, and when training as a nurse in London I went to all the 'Hops', 'Bops' and 'Balls'. I went for two reasons. Firstly, I enjoyed the dancing, pure and simple. Secondly, that was where you went to play the 'mating game'! If you had a boyfriend, dancing brought you physically closer. If you didn't, then this was the place to find one, either a partner for life or maybe just for the night. Drugs and drink were always available and dancing was an integral part of the scene.

New life in Christ always involves turning around from what is wrong in your life. It is not surprising that dancing was tainted for me. After I became a Christian, I thought it should be put completely out of my mind—that is, until I saw the Sacred Dance Group. They were part of the travelling group of musicians, singers and dancers called 'Shekinah', already mentioned. When I saw them dance in York Minster I longed with all my heart to dance again, this time for God.

Dancing may be part of our former life that we want to turn our backs on, but when we turn and face Jesus, he may give it back to us to use for his glory.

It would be marvellous if the only objections to dance as part of the Christian life were those I have mentioned above, objections that could fairly easily be refuted with good teaching. Unfortunately, whether or not to include dance in the Sunday service is a great deal more complicated than deciding the colour of the new robes for the choir. The very nature of dance sometimes results in the most easy-going of people being violently opposed to it, and discovering feelings of anger and resentment that seem to be out of all proportion to the matter in hand. When questioned they blush, and turn away mumbling something like, 'I personally never look at dance in church. I never find it helpful, it is just not for me.'

Some of us have very fixed ideas of who we are and how we worship and what God is going to be allowed to do in us. We feel safe with these ideas and we feel in control. Often when someone expresses these feelings about dance, they are also very guarded about allowing the Holy Spirit to work in their lives. A willingness to open up to the Holy Spirit, to allow him to do what he wills with our lives, often results in a readiness to be open to dance and to see it as a valuable part of our individual and corporate worship.

Why do some people find dance so difficult to look at? I think it could be that we are sometimes like the elder brother in the parable of the prodigal son. He came home from working in the fields to find music and dancing in his father's house because his younger brother had returned. He refused to enter and join in with the celebrations because he was jealous of this new-found relationship between his brother and his father. After all, he had faithfully slaved away year after year and never once had there been a party for him.

I have been just like the elder brother too. On one occasion, I remember coming away from a wonderful time of praise and worship in the church and saying to a friend, 'Well, honestly, there was so-and-so being told what a wonderful woman of God she is because she is so open to the Holy Spirit, and after all the hours I've spent counselling her.' In other words, I was jealous of the blessing given to someone whom I felt was unworthy of it, especially as I felt so far away from the Lord on that particular evening.

In fact, I can completely sympathize with all those who say, 'I personally never look, it's just not me.' The church I attended in London as a young Christian was strongly evangelical, with good sound teaching, but the worship that was encouraged was very private and personal. In other words, it wouldn't matter if there was no one else in the church, as long as there was me and my God. In complete contrast, when I moved to York I saw and heard prophecy, speaking in tongues, and I even saw people raise their hands in a church service and smile! I hated it all. I was frightened of such emotionalism. I objected to seeing other people 'showing off' their spirituality with such freedom, and wondered indignantly how anyone could dare to presume a knowledge of God's mind by actually speaking his word in prophecy to the whole congregation!

Then I changed. When, how or why I don't know. But I had a growing and unmistakable awareness of being filled with the Holy Spirit. As this happened I knew God was calling on me to repent. To repent of my resentment and my judgemental attitudes towards others, and to repent of being self-centred. He asked me if I really loved him with all my heart and soul and mind. He gave me a new love for himself. He also gave me a new love for my fellow Christians. Suddenly the most beautiful sight in the world for me was to see someone else caught up in adoration and worship of God. No matter how *I* felt, the fact that God was being worshipped and enjoyed by someone else was thrilling.

We must come to terms with our personal objections and face them in the light of God's word with the help of the Holy Spirit. We need to recognize where wrong attitudes are tainting our view of dance and ask God to give us his mind.

As a final word on facing the objections, here is a quote from an article in *The Church Reformer* in 1894:

> The art of dancing...perhaps more than all other arts, is an outward and visible sign of an inward and spiritual grace, ordained by the word of God himself, as a means whereby we receive the same, and a pledge to assure us thereof; and it has suffered even more than the other arts from the utter anti-sacramentalism of the British philistia. Your Manichean Protestant, and your superfine rabenalist, reject the dance as worldly, frivolous, sensual and so forth, and your dull stupid sensualist sees legs, and grunts with some satisfaction; but your sacramentalist knows something more than both of these. He knows what perhaps the dancer herself may be partially unconscious of, that we live now by faith and not by sight, and that the poetry of dance is the expression of unseen spiritual grace.

4. *Worship*

We have one of those modern alarm clocks that endeavours to wake us each morning with a quiet but persistent whine. Eventually its nagging call penetrates my brain, and with my eyes still closed I stagger across the room to switch it off. Then comes the most difficult decision of the day. Do I take pity on myself for having already been up in the night to feed the baby, crawl back into bed and wait for the children to wake me, or do I head for the kitchen to make tea? On a good day I make it to my desk, and armed with a mug of tea I open my Bible. Within three minutes my eyes are beginning to shut again, and if I am not careful my so-called Quiet Time is so quiet that I might as well still be in bed!

I don't know who coined the phrase 'Quiet Time', but whoever it was has done more harm than good. I am sure that he (or she) intended that 'quiet' should mean away from distracting influences, but unfortunately some of us are so quiet that, to an onlooker, we would appear to be in a deep sleep! If my special time alone with my husband consisted of me sitting slumped and motionless in a chair in front of him, I don't think we'd have a very good marriage, however hard I tried to conduct a good 'mental' relationship.

Those who wrote the Psalms probably would have been horrified to see the way most of us Christians spend time with the Lord! They would say to us, how can you really mean what you say if you don't put your whole self into it? How can you say 'Praise You' without flinging your arms in the air? How can you say 'I'm sorry, Lord' without flinging yourself on your face before him? The testimony of the Psalmist is that his 'Quiet Time' is *not* the biggest struggle of the day (as it is with so many of us). Instead he proclaims:

> It is good to give thanks to the Lord, to sing praise to thy name, O Most High; to declare thy steadfast love in the morning, and thy faithfulness by night, to the music of the lute and the harp, to the melody of the lyre. For thou, O Lord, has made me glad by thy work; at the works of thy hands I sing for joy. (Ps 92:1–4, RSV)

When was the last time your nextdoor neighbour complained about your singing at six o'clock in the morning? When was the last time the people in the flat below asked if you could take your shoes off before your morning celebration? When you meet your family at the breakfast table, are they aware that you have just been with someone you love? Do those at work see a smile on your face because it was with a smile that you greeted the Lord, before you greeted them? But, you say, my relationship with God isn't like that. 'Isn't it?' the Psalmist answers, 'Well, why not?'

Much has been written about worship, both personal

and corporate, and I would not pretend to have the last word on the subject. Unfortunately, it is very easy for us to read these books and to depersonalize what they are saying because the terminology that is used has become over-familiar to us. In other words, if I asked if you worshipped God, you probably wouldn't have any difficulty in giving an immediate answer in the affirmative. But if I asked if you were so in love with Jesus that you ached to sit at his feet and gaze into his eyes; if I asked you if you spent the day longing for the first opportunity to leave the chores, and to lie yourself prostrate before him, would it be so easy to answer 'yes'?

I think that some people are slightly shocked when they discover what the word 'worship' means in the New Testament in the original Greek. Actually, there are seven different Greek words for worship in the New Testament. Six occur only once. The seventh—*proskuneo*—comes sixty-six times, and it could be translated 'I come towards to kiss'. Why are we shocked? It is because we cannot conceive of such intimacy with God. An intimacy that involves not just our mind and spirit, but our whole being. So, worship does not only involve movement, and movement that is initiated by ourselves, but it involves the opening up of yourself that is necessary in order to kiss.

At the beginning of the Song of Solomon, it is a kiss that the maiden longs for. 'Let him kiss me with the kisses of his mouth: for thy love is better than wine.' In his book *The Song of Solomon*, Watchman Nee explains that this kiss is not the kiss of forgiveness—a kiss that all who belong to the Lord have already experienced, nor a kiss on the cheek like that of Judas Iscariot, nor a kiss upon the feet like that of Mary, but it is 'the kisses of his mouth', which would express a most personal and intimate love.

Does this sound like your 'Quiet Time'? Is this what worship means to you? If to worship is 'to come towards to kiss', then nothing is more natural than expressing that movement and that intimacy in dance. Your response to this question may be that it is all very well to talk of such ideals but, at six o'clock in the morning, you just don't feel like dancing! Jesus didn't tell us just to *feel* our love for God. His first *commandment* is recorded in Mark 12:30— 'Love the Lord your God with all your heart and with all your soul and with all your mind and with all your strength.' Worship that involves us totally is our first and foremost priority. It is the first action we should take when we come into God's presence. It is the first response we should make when we come to Christ. It is the first mark of the Holy Spirit in our lives (Gal 4:6) and was the first sign of the Holy Spirit at Pentecost. Worship is the ceaseless language of heaven. 'They never cease to sing, "Holy, holy, holy, is the Lord God Almighty"' (Rev 4:8, RSV). We were created to worship.

Do we in fact put *service* first and *worship* second? Do we spend so much time ministering to others that we forget to minister to the Lord? In the Old Testament we read how God set aside priests to do nothing else but minister to him. Ezekiel 44:15–16 says:

> But the Levitical priests, the sons of Zadok, who kept the charge of my sanctuary when the people of Israel went astray from me ... they shall approach my table, to minister to me, and they shall keep my charge (RSV).

God told his people that he wanted them to support these priests and to supply all their needs because they were doing *the* most important work—ministering to God. I have yet to come across a Christian church or fellowship who have set aside even one man, or woman, to do nothing but minister to the Lord! We give time, money, energy to his work, but do we give it to him?

I recently read a book about Mother Teresa's work in Calcutta. In spite of the desperate need, she and her nuns

spend one hour every morning and one hour every
evening in a time of 'Adoration'. Mother Teresa explains
that they are *not* social workers. Their first priority is to
worship God. When they have done *that*, they can go out
and serve his people.

Sadly, when someone we know *does* have their priorities
right, we so easily criticize them. Some years ago a cousin
told me she was considering becoming a nun. My first
thought was, 'What a waste of a life.' Remember Mary,
the sister of Martha and Lazarus, in the New Testament?
She had her priorities right but was criticized on two
occasions. John tells us how she 'wasted' on Jesus what
was probably her most precious possession, a pound of
costly perfume made of pure nard. Every time I read this
story, God says to me, 'Do you give me your most precious
possession, Judith?' I don't know about you, but for me
my most precious possession is my time. Three small
children, a home, and a travelling husband seem to take
up every available second. And yet I know that if only I
could learn to 'waste' time on God, he would take care of
everything else, with no trouble at all.

The other occasion when Mary was criticized was when
her sister Martha went to the Lord and said, 'Lord, do you
not care that my sister has left me to serve alone? Tell her
then to help me.' Luke tells us that Martha was 'distracted
with much serving'. I think that would be quite a good way
to describe me at about 5 p.m. every day! But the Lord
says to me exactly what he said to Martha. 'For goodness
sake, Judith, *stop* worrying about things that don't matter.
Just stop rushing round for five minutes and come and sit
at my feet. If only you could see that there is only *one*
thing that I really want you to do, and that is to worship
me. I'll help you with the tea and bathing the children,
when you have got your priorities right!'

Mary's example to us of 'wasting' her time and her
perfume on Jesus leads me on to the next question. Do I

ever do anything for God that has no other justification? Am I secure enough in my relationship with him to do something that doesn't bless anyone except him? At the heart of all true worship is the idea of sacrifice. My last question is, how much does my praise and worship rely on my feelings, instead of being a daily sacrifice of praise? Does my sacrifice cost me anything?

King David understood this. When he gave to God, he knew that he must give the best that he could afford, and more besides. When God told him to build an altar on the threshing floor of Araunah the Jebusite (2 Sam 24), he insisted on paying for the floor, in spite of the fact that Araunah was quite happy to give him not only the floor, but the oxen for the sacrifice and the wood for the fire! David said, 'No, but I will buy it off you for a price; I will not offer burnt offerings to the Lord my God which cost me nothing.'

Many of us go to church on Sunday and perhaps to a midweek prayer meeting, and don't find it too difficult to join in with the praise and worship. Please don't misunderstand me. It is wonderful when we can look forward to being with the body of Christ and praising God. Because we find it easy and a joy doesn't mean that it is worthless. But at six o'clock in the morning when we don't *feel* like praising God, and when there is no one else to see, God is thrilled when we 'waste' time on him just because we love him.

5.   *Try It, Try It, You Will See...*

I am sure that by now the reader is beginning to wonder if I am ever going to write about actually getting up on to one's feet and dancing, or if every chapter is going to be all theory and no practice. I hope you have stuck with me through the first four chapters. Dance is not something that is taught as a regular subject in our churches and fellowship, and I therefore felt it necessary to begin with the groundwork.

My children have a book in which one funny little character is trying to persuade another funny little character to eat 'green eggs and ham'. At last he says in despair, 'Try it, try it, you will see. You *will* like green eggs and ham.' This quote has now become part of our family life.

It works wonders with the children when one or other of them has convinced herself that she doesn't like her food. The answer comes back, 'Thank you, thank you, Sam-I-am. I *do* like your green eggs and ham.'

I must confess that at the beginning of this chapter I am very tempted to misquote this phrase: 'Try it, try it, you will see. You *will* like to dance!' When it comes to the crunch, unless you are willing to take a step of faith, no amount of theory will make any difference. What I want to do now is to give some idea of *how* to take those first few steps, and to give you a vision of what this could lead to.

Find somewhere quiet, away from all distracting influences, and at a time of day when you will be undisturbed. Now, don't just sit down on the nearest comfortable seat! Your usual way of coming into God's presence may be to sit with your head bowed and your hands together. This time, *kneel* on the floor, let your arms drop to your side, palms forward, and bow your head.

Why should this change of posture be so important?

One thing nearly all of us find difficult in our walk with the Lord is putting into practice in our lives things that we believe the Lord is speaking to us about. For example, we hear some teaching about reading the Bible more. We mentally agree with everything we hear, we fervently pray at the end of the talk that the Lord will help us to bring more discipline into our lives. But by the end of the week all we can say is, 'The spirit is willing, but the flesh is weak, once again, Lord, I have failed you.' Or in a time of prayer we *know* that God wants us to put a relationship right with someone we don't get on with. We say to ourselves, yes, I really *will* do it, and then nothing happens. Somehow, however firm our mental resolve, nothing seems to change. But if, instead of just the head being bowed in mental assent, the whole of the body is bowed, we are making a decision that comes from the heart as well as the mind. It is with our arms that we shall give a hug to that person we need to love. So let the arms say 'yes' to the Lord, as well as the head and the heart.

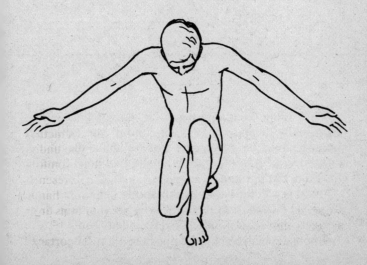

So, as we come before the Lord now, let us kneel. Let us pray, 'Lord, I don't want this time with you to be just lots of good ideas. I want my whole self to be submitted to you, and I am willing to accept whatever you want to say to me. Thank you, Lord, that you are my *father*. A father loves to see his children try out crazy things in front of him because they love him. Thank you that however silly I may look to myself, I never look silly to you.'

Now, before we go any further, we must 'check through' a few things with the Lord. This may take you a few minutes. It may take weeks. But we need to ask the Lord to show us if he wants to speak to us very specifically about the next few points. The reason they are so important is because they are major reasons why we might find difficulty in experiencing God's freedom:

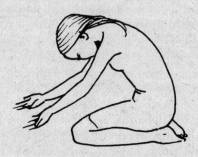

1.   This may seem very basic, but do you believe that God really loves *you*? 'Yes, of course,' you answer, 'I know he loves me because he gave his Son to die for me. Of course, he goes off me now and again. I don't think he *likes* me, but I'm sure he loves me.'

But this isn't the way the Bible speaks of God's attitude to us. The Bible tells us that God's love for us is more perfect, more true, more single-minded than any love relationship between two human beings. At the centre of our relationship with God is love. At the very centre of the Bible is a love song. It describes the love between a King and a maiden. It shows us how Christ loves the church, and it shows how God loves me, and how he wants me to love him in return. Our love relationship with Jesus should be more intimate, more passionate, more thrilling than any other relationship with anyone else.

God says to you, 'You are beautiful, my love.... You have ravished my heart, my sister, my bride.' Do you believe that you ravish the heart of Jesus? If your answer is that you are not good enough, remember that Jesus thought you were good enough to die for. And the beautiful white robe that you are wearing is God's gift to you to make you worthy of being 'beloved'.

Well, maybe God loves me on the inside, but look at me—I'm too fat, my hair needs a wash, and the baby was sick all down my skirt this morning. God doesn't mean he loves all those outside bits of me too.

What do you mean, doesn't love all those bits? He made you, didn't he? He created you, and with more love and tenderness than any mother ever lavished on her baby. He brought you into the world and cared for you when you were a child, and now he looks at the bald head, the double chin, the flat feet, and says, *you are beautiful*.

So let us begin with a prayer of repentance. 'Father, I'm sorry for not seeing the great love you have for me, and for not accepting myself as I am. Forgive me for being disrespectful of my body, and for thinking that I need to conform to the world's standards. Help me to remember I am not my own, I was bought with a price, and help me to glorify God in my body.

As you pray this prayer, raise your head, and look into the Lord's eyes, and *see* the love he has for you. And as you feel his love spread through your whole being—smile at him. You will thrill his heart.

2. This brings me to the second point, because it is possible that you don't really believe that you can do something that will truly thrill the heart of the Lord. I can remember the first time someone suggested to me I could actually minister to the Lord. I think I blushed because I was so embarrassed at the idea. I completely lacked the assurance that I could offer to God something worthy of him. Yet in Jesus we have been made perfect. It is through him that we have the confidence to approach God:

> For we have not a high priest who is unable to sympathise with our weaknesses, but one who in every respect has been tempted as we are, yet without sinning. Let us then with confidence draw near to the throne of grace, that we may receive mercy and find grace to help in time of need (Heb 4:15–16, RSV).

Jesus takes delight in seeing us worship. He has given us the Holy Spirit who will guide our thoughts, imagination, movements—all that we do—and direct them in ways that glorify God.

Psalm 134 calls us to bless the Lord:

> Come, bless the Lord
> all you servants of the Lord,

who stand by night in the house of the Lord!
Lift up your hands to the holy place,
and bless the Lord!
May the Lord bless you from Zion (rsv).

When we bless the Lord, he gives blessing to us too. As you humbly ask the Lord to accept the sacrifice of praise that you long to offer him, stand up before him, and imagine that you are gathering into your arms dozens and dozens of spring flowers. Take a step forward, and shower them at the feet of the Lord. Or cup your hands together, as if you were carrying a very precious bottle of perfume, and then empty it all on the Lord's feet.

I am quite sure that as you picture yourself in your imagination, you may feel very silly indeed. But you don't look silly to your Father.

3.   Thirdly, why is it you feel silly, and why do you hate this so much? The reason is pride. Pride makes us fearful of looking foolish and prevents us from doing something that will make us very vulnerable, exploring our relationship with God. As we begin to use movement, we have to

repent of our stubborn wills, and come to terms with
ourselves, facing up to our weaknesses and sin. The people
of Israel were often 'stiff-necked'. Let's pray now that the
Holy Spirit will show up any pride in our lives. It may be
that if you find it very difficult to be free before the Lord,
this physical stiffness is an indication of a stubborn will.
As you pray about, and confess, any pride within you,
bend down and touch the floor with your forehead, even
lie prostrate before the Lord. It will mean so much more
to both you and God than just saying it.

4.   The fourth reason for finding difficulty in experiencing
God's freedom is fear. Fear of what might happen if we let
the Holy Spirit take over our lives. Fear of being forced
into something that isn't us—something unreal. I think
some of us imagine that if we take that first step we will
suddenly find ourselves shod in fairy shoes that force us
to dance until we collapse in an exhausted heap. But our
heavenly Father, the giver of the Spirit of life, is one who
can always be trusted completely: 'Fear not, for I have
redeemed you; I have called you by name, you are mine'
(Is 43:1, RSV).

What have we to fear from one whose love is so great
for us? We may be fearful of something that will show us
our sin and the need to change, but if we resist the wind of
the Spirit that would flow through us and revolutionize
our lives, we will quench his work and lose him.

5.   If we are to find freedom in God's presence we must
be right in all areas of our life, not hiding anything from
God or from our brothers and sisters in Christ. The second
commandment was that we should love our neighbours as
ourselves. Maybe we need to repent about wrong attitudes
and upset relationships. We will find such release when
we seek out those with whom we have disagreed, and ask
forgiveness of them.

Whether a relationship has completely broken down,
or whether it is a case of just being 'out of sorts' with

someone, you may need to 'love' them before you can
'like' them. The best form of practical love is intercessory
prayer. The Bible is practical too. 'Bear one another's
burdens, and so fulfil the law of Christ' (Gal 6:2, RSV). As
you pray, imagine that you are holding the burdens of this
person in your hands. Walk forward, and imagine that
you are placing those difficulties and problems at the foot
of the cross. As you make this sacrifice for them, using
your whole body, God will give you the love for them that
you long for.

6. Finally, could it be that you and I are just plain
ignorant of the amazing riches that God is longing to
shower on us? We are so ignorant that we never think to
turn to him and say 'Yes, please'. Or, if not ignorant,
perhaps we have rather a low expectation of what God
can do and wants to do. A very basic example is Jesus'
promise to take away fear and to bring peace. We live
lives that we would never describe as fearless and peaceful,
because it never occurs to us to claim the victory that
Christ has already won. The relationship with Jesus that is
available to *every one of us,* is one of deep love, security
and joy.

Let us begin to ask the Lord right now to help us to live
in that victory. Instead of imagining that Jesus is only
interested in 'super-spiritual' Christians, let's begin to
move into that wonderful relationship of deep love that he
wants to have with all of us.

As you pray, bring your hands together with the palms
facing upwards, and imagine that you are holding out to
the Lord yourself, your family, your home, your work:
'Lord, I want you to take *everything* and to do with it what
you will.'

Now, raise your arms and hand everything over to God.
Now lift your face to him, and see again the love he has for
you. Now open your arms, and as you remove *every*
barrier between you and God, lay bare your whole self

before him, body, mind and spirit: 'Lord, *this* is how I want to be before you, now and every day.'

You may not have realized it, but what you are beginning to do is to use your body in your relationship with God. You are beginning to dance.

There is so much more to discover, and as we submit ourselves to God in dance, we begin to find that he ministers to us in a new and exciting way. Just one final word, though, before we go on to explore many more areas where movement can be used. Please don't imagine that I am writing this only for young, fit and healthy bodies. Since my first pregnancy, I have suffered from intermittent back pain, although it is usually not very severe. About two weeks ago I was suddenly aware that I could feel it again and, while writing this chapter, it has been more painful than ever! So when I have suggested movements, it has been with the knowledge that I probably can't carry them out myself with ease or comfort! I have had to learn to respect my body. In spite of pain and disability, even if you are confined to a wheelchair, I believe that your dancing for the Lord can be the most beautiful and treasured gift in the Lord's eyes.

With my hands lifted high,
I will praise thee, O Lord!

6. *Keep Going—There Is Much More to Explore!*

A couple of years ago I travelled to a small village up in the Yorkshire Wolds in order to visit a ladies' prayer group. They had asked me to come and lead an afternoon of dance. It nearly always happens that it is only when I arrive at a meeting that I have any idea of the numbers who will be present, or of the floor space that is available for us in which to move.

On this occasion there were about ten ladies rather tightly packed into the front room of a blacksmith's cottage. They were all wonderful Christian women whose only desire was to know more of Jesus, and I think I sensed right at the beginning that God was going to work powerfully, in spite of the fact that I had no idea what I was going to do in such a small space.

After some introductory teaching, I suggested that we should turn to the Song of Solomon. We asked the Holy Spirit to take hold of our imaginations and to use them for God's glory. Each of us imagined that we were the bride dancing before the Bridegroom. I think that the Lord gave us a glimpse of what it will be like to be in heaven, and each of us knew that even now the Lord was saying to us, 'Behold you are beautiful, my love; behold you are beautiful; your eyes are doves my beloved, truly lovely.' I think it was one of the most amazing times of dance I have ever had before the Lord, and yet we only had room to raise our heads and to do one or two very simple arm movements.

That afternoon spent with those ladies showed me just how exciting it can be to meditate on a verse, or even a few words from the Bible. Through such meditation, God can sometimes speak to us more powerfully than at any other time, and if we are willing to be really free before him, we will find a greater communion with him than perhaps ever before.

In this chapter I want to explore all the different and exciting ways of using dance and movement for you as an individual, or for you as part of a prayer group. I shall begin by explaining more about meditation—something that many of us find difficult.

First of all we must ask ourselves why the word 'meditation' makes us want to run a mile! We dismiss it as something only the spiritual giants ever attempt. We are convinced that in order to meditate one needs enormous powers of concentration, and tremendous mental ability. You know, I think we sometimes assess someone's spirituality by the level of their IQ! We are *so* unbalanced in our view of the whole human being (i.e. *big* head, little everything else) that we imagine that our growth as Christians is stunted because we are not intellectual enough.

We say to ourselves, 'If I was more clever, I could grasp more easily everything there is to know about God. If I had more concentration, and a better memory to learn my Bible verses, I could spend hours in meditation; then I could become a *first*-class Christian rather than a second-class Christian.'

Surely it can't be true that anyone is excluded from any of the good things that Christ offers us just because of an intellect that is slower than others' to understand things. I think that meditation is one of these 'good things'. Jesus said, 'Unless you become like little children, you cannot enter the kingdom of God.' Children aren't clever, but they aren't afraid of using their imaginations. We need to be more childlike in our approach to our relationship with the Lord, with no fear of using our imagination and of acting out what we imagine.

My five-year-old daughter gave us an example of this very recently. We always hold hands round the table when we say grace before a meal. On one occasion she said to her three-year-old sister, who was sitting next to her, 'Hold hands with Jesus, Anna.' They both shut their eyes and held up clenched fists. When the meal had begun, a friend who was eating with us asked whose hands they had been holding. 'Jesus', of course', came back the reply. Are we so sure that they were just pretending?

The best way to learn about meditation is to do it. Look at John 15:1: 'I am the true vine, and my Father is the vinedresser' (RSV). Read the verse through, and then begin with a prayer. 'Lord, I offer this time to you. I want to come into your presence, to be *with* you, not just to learn *about* you. May this time be a time when you, Lord, lead the way, and I follow step by step. Thank you that if I am honestly listening, you are alwasy ready to speak to me. I offer you my whole self, body mind and spirit.'

It is important to ask the Holy Spirit to take control of your imagination and then *trust* that he will—and do not be frightened of it. God gave you your imagination for a purpose. It is not just something that needs to be stamped on because it takes us away from so-called 'reality'. The pastor Alex Buchanan allows the Spirit to use his imagination to give him an amazing insight into the spiritual world. When Alex describes how he sees God sitting in the heavenly places, I am aware of how *real* the description is. This isn't speculation. It's the Holy Spirit using a man's imagination for the very purpose that God gave it to him.

So, with a sense of expectancy and excitement at what God has in store for you, read through the verse again, and 'wait' on God. Because we are all individuals and loved by God, no two people will be led along the same path.

When I lead a dance workshop in a time of meditation, I ask each person to share briefly what God has shown them. Here is a testimony from such an occasion:

As I read through the verse, the picture that came into my mind was of a vineyard. The word that stood out for me more than any other was 'true'. When I moved closer in my mind to the vineyard, I saw that although from a distance all the plants looked real, they were in fact all plastic. Just like those displays of greenery that you see in office buildings—such a let-down when you get close enough to see the dust! I seemed to spend ages just thinking about the dust on plastic plants, so I had to ask the Holy Spirit to show me what the Lord was speaking to me about. Suddenly I realized that in the centre of the vineyard there was a beautiful, tall vine, reaching to the sky. In order to get to it I needed to pull up the plastic plants. The Lord said to me quite plainly that I needed to 'pull up' some wrong things in my life, in order to be properly cleaved to him, and able to bear fruit.

I asked him to show me what these things are, and in my imagination I saw little tags on the plastic plants. So I moved across the room and I was able to imagine pulling these sins out of my life, as I pulled the plants up out of the ground, asking for the Lord's forgiveness, and then throwing them behind me. When I reached the vine at the centre, I reached out my hand and grasped the stem of the vine. I felt such relief and love for Jesus flow through me that I wanted to dance for you. So I did!

The way to encourage a group of people to praise the Lord in dance is with meditation as just described. In order to take our minds off ourselves, and in order to be less self-conscious, we need to fill our thoughts and imaginations with Jesus—just as in the testimony above, where the person was so overcome with the love of Jesus and so forgetful of herself, that she 'took off' in praise and worship.

But please don't imagine for one minute that if you had been watching this girl dance, you would have suddenly seen her move with the confidence and grace of a professional dancer. Or indeed, don't imagine that she herself didn't feel awkward and clumsy. Most of us, when we leave childhood, lose the ability to 'let go' with our bodies. With God's help we can rediscover it, but it takes time and the discipline to persevere.

It is surprising how many people will persevere during a dance workshop, but as soon as they try to praise God in dance in their own private times of worship, they give up with frustration at their own inability. It is as if, after one lesson of the violin, I went home and tried to play the Beethoven Violin Concerto. One of the best ways of discovering more freedom in worship, is to play a worship tape or record over and over again until it is so familiar that the words and music are second nature. Then enjoy spending half an hour actually working out some movements. It doesn't matter how obvious they seem to be, or how simple. In fact, the more simple the better. This isn't wasting time. It is creating an offering of praise for God.

I have often found that as we go into a time of worship as a group, it is helpful to sing the same chorus again and again. In this way, each individual can repeat movements if they have found them helpful, and therefore become more released and free. But whether you are working as part of a group, or as an individual alone with God, step out in faith, because God has *much, much* more waiting for you than just stumbling through simple beginnings. Perhaps one of the reasons that dance can be so misunderstood is that many of us haven't dared to take it any further than the occasional hop up and down during a festival of praise. But there is nothing superficial about God's relationship with us, even if we are guilty of being superficial with him.

Step out in faith, and God will reveal himself to you as you abandon your *whole* self to him. Meditate on the Song of Solomon and allow Jesus to lead you into a deep, intimate and sweet relationship that knows no bounds. Ask yourself this question now: do you love Jesus just because of what he has done for you, or do you love him for himself, because he is the One 'whom your soul loves'? Are you sometimes 'sick with love' for him? Can you say, with the maiden in the poem, 'His speech is most sweet, and he is altogether desirable. This is my beloved, and this is my friend'?

There is no greater joy than dancing before such a lover. And as I give myself to him in adoration, he touches me in the deepest parts of my being. He gives me his peace, the peace that really does pass all understanding. He gives me his joy, the joy that brings strength. He heals my fear—how can I be afraid if God himself calls me his beloved?

I believe that God gave us the physical relationship between a husband and his wife in order to show us how he wants our love to be with him. When a couple come together in love, they give themselves to one another in

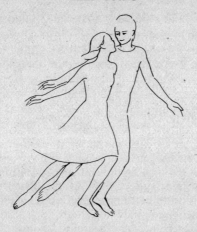

body, mind and spirit. The result of that union is a deeper love for one another, as well as a deep sense of peace and joy. Making love doesn't do away with the troubles of the world, but it helps me to see them in their right perspective! There is healing in sexual love. Jesus wants us to experience that peace and joy, that healing in our love relationship with him. But he can't give it to us if our relationship with him is shallow. How can he heal the tension of worry in the back of your neck or how can he heal that knot of fear in your stomach if you don't offer your body to him?

The gift of love between a man and a woman is available to some of us. The gift of love between Jesus and each one of his children is available to *all* of us. If you will use your body in your relationship with him, if you will express your pain and sorrow, your longings and desires, your repentance and joy at forgiveness, then Jesus will be able to minister to you in a way you have never experienced before. If you will dance before him in praise and worship, you will find the healing and the peace and joy that truly passes all understanding.

I recently spent a morning with a lady called Kay whom I have known for many years, and who initiated the dance group in the fellowship where I belong. She told me of how the Lord has worked in her life through dance:

My own first conscious 'dance before the Lord' came from a 'spring of joy' (Ps 87:7) as God called me to be available to his people—the church. I danced to him in my room and it was thrilling to discover how acceptable this was to him.

I later realized that the source of that spring had first revealed itself to me in a time of grief. Words were too difficult and my appeals, demands, dependence and weakness were most often expressed in quite powerful bodily movement.

I found this to be an important release of emotions that enabled me to receive comfort, healing and acceptance from my heavenly Father, and deepened my love for him and relationship with him.

The Lord will also work very powerfully through movement and dance in a prayer group. Judy was someone who, for many months, had been unable to come to church. There was much within the fellowship that she could not accept, and when she did eventually attend a service, relationships were strained. In the dance workshop, one evening, we were expressing through movement how Jesus will go out into the wilderness to bring back one stray lamb to the fold. Somehow Judy was the one who was being drawn back to the body, and suddenly we all realized that this wasn't just an exercise. As we reached out to her she broke into sobs, and through the actual movement of being drawn in among us, the division between herself and the church was healed.

God has also ministered to me through dance. Two years ago he was able to heal me of a literally 'gut rotting' fear. I say 'gut rotting' because that was exactly the way that this fear affected me. When people talk about their insides going to jelly, I know exactly what they are talking about! It had gone on for months, and affected my whole life. I had prayed and prayed, and many others had prayed for me. Then one Sunday evening, when everyone else in the house had left for church and I had put the children to bed, the Lord told me very clearly to *leave* the washing-up and to dance for him. As I ministered to him in dance, he healed me as specifically as if I had been suffering from a cancer. For the first time in nearly a year, I felt peaceful, really, really peaceful. When I looked back, I realized that during that time of fear and doubt, I hadn't danced for God once. I had agonized before him in prayer, I had tried to hand everything to him, but until I 'let go' with my whole self, God wasn't able to work a miracle in me.

Now on this occasion I had known without any shadow of doubt what it was that had been causing this inner disease. I could relate it all back to a television programme about 'the Bomb'. But sometimes Satan is a lot more

subtle. You might sense that something is wrong somewhere, but it has gone on for so long that you have learned
to live with it. Well, I suggest that first you confess to the
Lord that the reason you aren't a particularly powerful
soldier in his army is that you have been using an
excuse to keep you in sick bay. Ask him to show you what
is wrong, and ask him to show you what is causing the
disease. (When I use the word 'disease', I don't mean
measles or smallpox, I mean dis-ease, i.e. not being quite
right somewhere!)

Now thank the Lord for his tender love, and begin to
praise him in dance. As you move, you will soon be aware
in what particular part of your body you are just 'not
comfortable'. For example, many of us are stiff across our
shoulders and in the back of our necks. I know I can go for
days on end like this, and it is only when I come to dance
for God that I realize something is wrong. The something
that is wrong is, of course, that I am carrying on my
shoulders some problem or some care that I should have
handed over to the Lord days ago. The last time that I did
this, the Lord showed me just how much writing this book
was worrying me! I needed to confess that worry, and
actually to 'feel' God lift it from my shoulders. The release
was amazing. Up until then I had no idea how much I had
been trying to complete the book in my own strength.

Your body will reflect, in one way or another, fears,
resentments and worries, even wrong relationships. By
'offering' your body to the Lord in dance, he will be able
to show you what is wrong, *and* he will be able to heal you.

Another very exciting way of using movement is in
intercession, and once again this can be for an individual
or for a group. Sometimes we cry to the Lord for someone
we love very much, but words seem inadequate to express
the desperation in our heart. Perhaps this person doesn't
yet know God, or perhaps he or she needs healing in body
or mind. I thank God for the gift of tongues, because

the Lord helps me to intercede for someone by speaking in tongues. I also thank him for the gift of dance, because when I care very deeply about someone or something, I want to put my *whole* self into expressing that care. When we pray we need to ask God in what direction he wants our prayers to go. If you ask him, he will give you movements that will express his will in a situation. For example, I long with all my heart for a certain couple to come to know Jesus, and as soon as I bring their names before the Lord, I feel the Holy Spirit bending not just my knees, but my whole body until I am prostrate on the floor. The Lord is telling me that I must be willing to lay down my life for the couple, to be ready to serve them in whatever way the Lord asks me.

Try a very simple movement with me now. Think of someone whom you long to come to know Jesus. Clench your hands very tightly together in front of you, and pray:

'Father, this is how his [or her] life is, shut away from the warmth of your love. Please, Lord, soften his heart so that he responds to your word.' As you pray, begin very gently to unclench your hands, and open up your fingers, as a flower will open up to the warmth of the sun. Continue to pray in faith that this person's life will respond to God's love in the same way. Keep the movement going until your arms are stretched up and your hands are apart. Now give thanks to the Lord that this person's life *is* going to be released to God in the same way. Hallelujah! Whenever I pray for someone like this, my faith is increased dramatically, and I leap for joy with the excitement of it all!

It was during a dance workshop when we were discovering more about interceding with movement that God spoke very clearly to a friend of mine, Jill. As she began to dance before the Lord, she wasn't initially sure for whom he wanted her to pray. She asked the Holy Spirit to guide her movements, and after a few minutes she realized that her hands kept returning to the area around the back of her head and her neck. Her mother had been ill for some months, and Jill suddenly saw in her mind her mother using exactly the same movements when she was in pain. 'God was simply telling me,' said Jill, 'that he wanted me to pray for my mother.' The next movements were very big, encompassing gestures that seemed to take in Jill, and her mother, and the whole family. 'God was showing me that he had *everything* in control. He wasn't necessarily going to heal my mother, but he understood and knew everything we were going through.' Jill's mother eventually died of a disease associated with the brain, and I remember that when it happened, Jill radiated a love and a peace that could *only* come from God. He was in control as he had promised.

7. *Congregational Dance*

The uses of dance in church

Celebration

Praise the Lord!
Praise God in his sanctuary;
Praise him in his mighty firmament!
Praise him for his mighty deeds;
Praise him according to his exceeding
    greatness!

Praise him with trumpet sound;
Praise him with lute and harp!
Praise him with timbrel and dance;
Praise him with strings and pipe!
Praise him with sounding cymbals,
Praise him with loud clashing cymbals,
Let everything that breathes, praise
   the Lord!
Praise the Lord!

If only we Christians would realize that such exhortation is not to be taken heed of just once a year, or even once a month. To rejoice and to celebrate should be a part of every Christian's day. When I was a child, my father used to tease me that life for me was one long party! As followers of Christ we know that life is *not* one long party. When we come into fellowship with Jesus we enter into his sufferings. Apart from anything else, our eyes are opened to the evil in the world, and our hearts are truly burdened for those who suffer, and for those who don't know the love of God.

Nevertheless, when we look at the cross, we know that from pain and suffering comes victory. We weep with Jesus as we work for him in the world, but we also celebrate with him that the victory has been won and that he is in control.

Whatever our circumstances, we give God a sacrifice of praise. But worship should not just be personal—it is very much a corporate activity. What better way to celebrate the victory of the cross, our new life in Christ and our fellowship in the body, than with dance?

Praise and thanksgiving, however, is not the whole story. There are other reasons why dance is so important to the corporate life of every church and fellowship.

Encouraging fellowship

Have you ever heard the phrase 'Christians who pray together, stay together'? I should like to precede it with 'Christians who dance together, pray together'.

Have you ever been in a prayer meeting when someone has suggested holding hands? The effect can be electric, and the embarrassment acute. However, the simple movement of reaching out your hand to someone else can actually unlock a spirit of commitment and love, maybe even a healing in the relationship. Kneeling in a circle and holding hands together indicates openness to one another and a unity together. It could confirm your prayer time as never before.

So, if holding hands in a circle has so much effect, how much more dancing together as a church? We had a very special time for over a year in our church in York, when Sunday after Sunday the whole congregation gathered together for lunch and afterwards sang and danced together. Those of us who led the dance group taught Israeli dances, one or two by the Fisherfolk, and some simple circular dances we had choreographed ourselves.

Those who didn't join in sat at the side and sang and clapped. My grandmother was staying with us for the summer. She couldn't actually dance, but she often said how wonderful it was to dance through the feet of others, and to experience the sense of community that the dancing brought about.

Why did we choose Israeli, as opposed to, say, English country? Recently I saw a display by a teacher of Israeli folk dance. She herself was using movements passed down in the tradition, and may well have been oblivious to their meaning as worship. But for me, it was a spiritual experience just watching her. It was like the Old Testament come to life!

Afterwards when we chatted together she told me that

Israeli dancing is one of the few types of ethnic dance that is still vital and alive. It is a living tradition. New dances are being created all the time. Those who teach and choreograph spend as much time in Israel as possible to research new dances and to keep close to their roots.

Preserved through 1,100 years of dispersion, their dance is flourishing as never before in the modern state of Israel. Is it not possible that the flourishing of their folk dancing has something to do with the long-awaited return to their homeland?

So, dance encourages fellowship and builds up the body of Christ. It also encourages us to laugh at one another when we tread on each other's toes! As we dance we cannot help but lose some of our fear and mistrust of one another.

Weapon in spiritual battle

Dance is also a weapon in the spiritual battle. As we offer a sacrifice of praise in dancing, we soon discover its power in our battle to resist the devil and stand firm in the Lord. It is very hard to cling on to feelings of self-pity, resentment, loneliness, etc. or to give room to the devil's attacks of doubt and fear, if we are prepared to offer ourselves freely to God in movement. It is perhaps because of its value in asserting very positively our faith in God that Jesus said:

> Blessed are you when men hate you, and when they exclude and revile you, and cast out your name as evil, on account of the Son of man! Rejoice in that day, and leap for joy (Lk 6:22–23, rsv).

When we affirm what is in our heads and our hearts with our bodies too, then great things will begin to happen. Actions speak louder than words, we say. Yesterday I was talking to a leader of a fellowship near York where the

Lord is working powerfully. He told me of an occasion when the Lord brought prophetic words to the people. The Lord said: 'Bow yourselves before me', and they responded quietly in their hearts. And then it came again: 'Bow yourselves before me'. So everyone prayed more fervently to abase themselves. Yet again it came. Suddenly everyone realized that God didn't just want an assent that was 'spiritual'. He wanted them to respond with their whole selves. Almost as one, the entire congregation fell down before God in awe and wonder.

When God speaks to us, we must be obedient and respond. He doesn't just ask for half a response, he asks for complete obedience.

You may object that what happened in that church was not dance. But the freedom they had to respond to God in that way was almost certainly tied to the fact that they were a dancing fellowship in their praise and worship.

When we use movement and dance to come before the Lord, in repentance or thanksgiving, we 'ink in' what is in our hearts before God, man and the devil.

Evangelistic use of dance

It is through our praise and worship that God becomes more clearly visible to outsiders:

> He put a new song in my mouth, a song of praise to our God. Many will see and fear, and put their trust in the Lord (Ps 40:3, RSV).

Dance is a visual expression of that praise, and is one of the most powerful ways of witnessing to the life of the Spirit. The reality of God's existence, inspiring the faith of those who hold nothing back from God in their praise, and who even present their bodies to him, becomes hard to dispute.

Dancing also expresses something of what God is like. Instead of worship that is still, dry and colourless, making

God seem very boring to the outsider, God can be seen as the creator of life, movement, beauty and sensitivity. It also reflects the fruit of the Spirit—his peace, joy, gentleness, love, self-control—in a way that words alone cannot.

Movement used to bring healing

I have already spoken of how powerful dance is for an individual and for a group, to bring to the surface and heal hurts, fears and tensions. When the whole church participates in dance, either through actually dancing or 'dancing through the feet of others', needs can be released to God, and his love can be received.

Dance brings reality in our relationships together. So often we need one another to 'speak the truth in love', to recognize things in us that need to change, and many times we will be faced by the reality of this need when we dance together. It is impossible to dance with someone against whom you are holding a resentment!

When all are dancing, and you look around you, you are going to *see* one another's relationship with God. This is a time when you really need to trust. It is a time of very great vulnerability. Either we criticize and harden our hearts, or we grow together in acceptance, freedom and wholeness.

Taking the first step

So, how do you begin? You may be thinking that it depends an awful lot on who you are. That you are not even an elder, let alone the vicar, and that there is not even a remote possibility that anyone will listen to you—however excited you are. But this is man's point of view, not God's. There may be a power structure in your church, but in God's eyes each one of us is as important in the body as any other. You just might be the person whom God has chosen to bring a vision of dance and movement to your church or fellowship.

So, your first job is to pray. You need to ask God if he is going to give you a gift of dance yourself, or lead you into the ministry of dance, or if you will be someone in the church who will encourage and support any dance that happens. Through prayer God may also show you problems and fears in your fellowship that need to be healed, so that when movement *is* introduced there won't be too much of an uproar!

Pray that God will pour out his Spirit afresh on the congregation so that people will be ready for new freedom, new vision. Pray especially for the leaders, that they will be truly open to learn new and exciting things from the Lord. Remember that dancing is a great 'leveller' and this could be quite a challenge to a leader!

Next, you need to ask the Lord what is *his* vision and *his* will for your church. Visit other churches to see how powerful dance can be, but please, please don't try to institute something in your own fellowship just because it looked good somewhere else.

Whether you call your weekly encounter with the rest of the body of Christ a worship service, or a fellowship meeting, one way of thinking about it is to see it as a tapestry. A tapestry carefully woven with many beautiful threads, and offered as praise to the Lord. Each one of us is a thread, each one of us a slightly different colour from all the others and each one of us utterly necessary to make up the picture. Also, the different offerings and gifts that we bring interweave together until the picture is complete.

Preaching and teaching, singing and playing instruments, banner-making and flower arranging, collecting the offering and stewarding, all are parts of the order of the tapestry. The creator of the picture is the Holy Spirit, and each tapestry, like each snowflake, is different.

In likening the worship service to a tapestry, it becomes

easier to understand that each part, or thread, is as necessary as any other part. The early church used the word 'liturgy' to describe the different parts of the service for much the same reason. 'Liturgy' comes from the word *leitorgia* which was the public work each person did to build and repair roads and bridges and other works for the community and its growth. The different parts of the liturgy are all necessary and all dependent on one another.

Ask the Holy Spirit exactly how he wants to fit dance into your 'tapestry' or liturgy. Perhaps the first people to dance in your church should be the children. Perhaps the Holy Spirit wants to open people up to movement by using simple hand movements to a well-known chorus. Perhaps your numbers are small enough to meet in a large room, where a simple circular dance could be possible. You may come from a High Anglican or Catholic tradition with a very formal liturgy, and dance could be incorporated into the procession or the recession. It might be that God wants every member of your fellowship to dance, or he may be calling a small number into a group ministry so that the main body can dance through the feet of a few.

I shall go on in the next chapter to explain what it means to have a ministry of dance. In your church the Holy Spirit may call a whole group to minister and to lead. On the other hand, there might be just one person, perhaps in the choir, to whom the Lord has already given a gift of leading in worship and who might encourage the whole church to use their bodies in their relationship with God.

The building you use for corporate worship may well be unsuitable for some of the things described here. If so, I can only urge you to do what you can in the space you have, and perhaps pray for the day when the fixed seating can be removed.

Having established that the beginnings of dance in your church might be quite unlike anything you have seen or heard of before, here are some basic guidelines to help you start.

However you begin, you must be sure of the backing of the leader or leaders of the church. This may seem obvious. Surely if the leader has said I can teach the children a simple dance for Easter Sunday, he *must* be giving me headship? Unfortunately this isn't always the case. I have heard of occasions when the vicar has said yes to dance in the service (either by the whole congregation or by a small group) and then when there has been opposition, has left the initiator of the dance to 'carry the can'. It may be that some special teaching from the pulpit is needed before any sort of movement can take place. Teaching on worship, teaching on self-acceptance, teaching on freedom and openness, all these things need to be stressed over and over again as the first steps of dance are introduced.

Then, begin with the children. Even if you never get anywhere else with congregational dancing, you will find that God will use the children and their simple offering of dance very powerfully. The children themselves will grow in the Lord as they praise him in dance, and interpret songs they know well. The congregation will be ministered to, and a deeper understanding of being one family in the Lord will inevitably grow. It is very difficult not to be challenged by the faith of the children, and by their simplicity and their freedom.

At this point, if at all possible, begin to involve everyone. People are much less critical if even in a very small way they are taking part themselves, perhaps clapping or singing along. We have one or two dances in our church that the congregation has seen so often that many people begin to break into the arm movements as the song begins. Two of our favourites are 'Arise, shine, for your light has come', and 'We cry hosanna, Lord'. When these dances were originally choreographed, they were kept deliberately static with many lovely arm and hand movements. Therefore they can be danced as easily by someone in a wheelchair, as by those sitting in the pews.

It is amazing that once the children have begun to move, many people who previously would have been horrified at the idea of dance in church begin to relax and are even open to joining in themselves. From now onwards, the possibilities are endless.

Here are some ideas. At the point in the service where the Lord's Prayer is said, join hands in order to affirm that he is *our* Father. Then raise hands, still joined, on the words 'hallowed be thy name' to show that our worship comes out of our unity together. On the words 'as we forgive those who sin against us', drop hands on to the shoulders of the person standing in front of you, as a sign of giving and receiving forgiveness.

Asking for the help of the Holy Spirit, add very simple movements to other well-known prayers in the service, so that people come to learn them and thus become more free and relaxed.

Incorporate a very simple prayer walk into the first or the last hymn of the service. This is particularly helpful if people can be encouraged to leave their pews and follow

either up or down the aisles. The best step is the tripodium
step, which in fact was the most common dance step in
Christian church processions for a thousand years, and fits
with any hymns of 2/4, 3/4 or 4/4 time. This step is simply
three steps forward and one back, three steps forward,
and one back. Arms can be raised in an attitude of worship
or linked so that you move two or three abreast. When I
first learned this 'prayer walk' it was as an Israeli dance,
and we placed our right hand on the shoulder of the
person in front. The great advantage of this is that it
enables people to join in as and when they wish.

I have already mentioned Israeli dancing to encourage
fellowship. It is a good idea to hold a series of workshops
in order to teach Israeli dancing to the congregation. If
you have the space, dancing outside the church before
and after the service is a wonderful witness to the
community in which you live. I can remember at the end
of an Easter communion service, the doors at the back of
the church were thrown open wide, and the whole congregation followed the dance group out into the city where
we all danced or sang in praise to Jesus.

I shall talk more about holding workshops in the next
chapters and the Appendix, but there is no doubt that the
best congregational dance happens following a series of
workshops. A couple of months before a special service,
encourage as many people as possible from the fellowship
to come to such a series in order to put together a dance
for this service. Some of the most wonderful dancing I
have ever seen has come together like this. If this happens
often enough, different members of the congregation may
dance on different occasions.

I think the ideal combination of dance in the 'tapestry'
of the worship service is as follows:

1.   A very simple dance (up and down the aisles if that is
all the space that you have) done by twenty or thirty

members of the congregation.

2. A more complex dance done by three, four or five members of a dance group.

3. One or two songs with simple arm movements in which the whole congregation can join.

As a final note on congregational dance, I must not forget to mention what is sometimes called the 'Holy Hop'. This is when a group of Christians become so excited about the Lord that they cannot keep still and jig from one foot to another. It is a great start, although a word of warning is necessary. It is very easy for a fellowship to become blasé about such dancing until it is nothing more than 'the thing to do' at certain times in a service, and ceases to be in any way glorifying to God. It also very easily results in people 'doing their own thing', sometimes from entirely the wrong motives.

In the same way that it is usually wrong for people to use their gift of tongues individually in a worship service, because it does not edify the whole body, it can be wrong for individuals to suddenly 'take off' in dance, unless the Lord is specifically asking them to use the dance to minister to his people as well as to himself.

When the whole congregation is inspired to dance for the Lord, the result will be something that is beautiful in its harmony and its order, as when the Spirit moves a gathering of people to sing in tongues together. At such times we have just a small glimpse of the coming joy of being together with the Lord in heaven.

8. *Dance Ministry*

While I believe that dance can be and should be a part of the life of every Christian, young or old, healthy or infirm, Catholic or Protestant, obviously only a few are called into the *ministry* of dance. So you might be tempted to give the next few pages a miss.

Please don't! In the first place *you* may have a call but not be aware of it yet. Secondly, if the Lord is going to use dance as a powerful ministry in the church, as he is already beginning to, then as many people as possible need to understand it from the beginning. They can then give the encouragement, love and support needed from all sides as the first few faltering steps are taken.

What is a ministry of dance?

At the end of the last chapter, I mentioned an ideal combination of dance in the worship service: arm movements for everybody to do with one or two worship songs; something simple in the way of folk dance for possibly twenty or thirty; and a set piece done by the smaller dance group on their own.

It is the ministry of the 'small dance group' that I want to concentrate on in this chapter.

But why have a special dance 'ministry'? Doesn't this create an exclusive group who are set apart from everyone else? Isn't it enough if the whole congregation dance?

No, it isn't enough, because God has a special work to do through those with specific gifts in dance. And yes, it does set some people apart, in the same way that the choir or singing group is made up of those with special musical gifts, or church wardens are those with gifts of looking after the church building and welcoming people into it.

A ministry of worship

What is the special work that God wants the dance group to do for him? It is to worship him. The first and foremost purpose of a Christian dancer is to praise and worship God. It is also a ministry to man, but first it is a ministry to the Lord. Just as the Israelites set aside priests and priestesses to minister unto the Lord day and night in the temple, so the dance group comes together to praise and magnify God.

This is the duty and joy of every Christian, to be sure, but let's be clear: the ministry of dance is utterly dependent on this basic motive and sense of serving and pleasing God through worship.

Secondly, it is a ministry of leading the rest of the body of Christ into greater praise and adoration. Whether the dance is carefully choreographed or a spontaneous response to a sense of God's special presence in a service, its purpose is to open the windows of heaven so that God's people might have a greater vision of him in all his glory.

Here is the testimony from a man for whom the dance ministry in a church has meant a great deal as a means of worshipping God:

> One thing I am not, is emotional. I find it quite difficult to be in a service when everyone around me is 'lost in wonder, love and praise'. My mind gets in the way. But once or twice, when the dance group have been worshipping God, I have been so lifted out of myself that I have found it difficult not to leap out of the pew too!

Another lady said to me once:

> I felt so down through most of the service—I couldn't seem to enter into any sort of worship. And then suddenly, during the last hymn, a dancer came down the aisle and ran up to the front of the church, praising the Lord. She was so full of praise and joy that I broke down and tears streamed down my face. The love of Jesus was suddenly so real to me.

Yet another comment:

> The dancing is a catalyst in the worship. I don't know how it works, but when the group ministers in dance, we seem to move up into the heavenly places.

A prophetic ministry

The dance ministry is also, to some extent, a prophetic ministry. It is prophetic because through it God speaks to his people. Sometimes the lessons that we learn together can only be expressed and received through movement and dance. This seems particularly so in the area of relationships. Dance speaks directly to people's hearts, sometimes breaking down prejudices and barriers and encouraging people to receive or recognize things in themselves that words have failed to touch.

Over and over again we have found in our dance group in York that the dance created for a service dovetails perfectly with the combined message of the preaching, the singing, the music, the banners, etc. It is the Holy Spirit who gives movements as we plan a dance, and it is he who makes what we create part of what the Lord is saying to the church on a particular occasion.

Here is part of a dance that has spoken volumes to those who have seen it. It is set to a song written for Northern Ireland:

> The two dancers come from opposite corners, turning in graceful circles, and face each other in the centre. Their hands approach, touch and close around those of the other. The smiles on their faces, and in their eyes, full of love and acceptance, complete the interpretation:

> Come, Lord Jesus
> With healing hands
> To bind us together
> In unity.

(From 'Come, Lord Jesus' by Diane Davis Andrews, © Celebration Services.)

It is more essential now than ever before that the Lord's

word should come to us through dance and drama. Increasingly, people are deaf to words. Other forms of communication are vital in our visual age of television, films and video. When dance is used to interpret songs, sometimes grown too familiar with use, it can bring new meaning and reality to the words.

An evangelistic ministry

I have already mentioned, in preceding chapters, what a powerful witness dance can be to the non-Christian. It is important to emphasize, too, how much the dance group can communicate to the world not only the extent of God's love for us but how much he has taught us to love one another. Two people dancing together must have an open relationship, and this is so obvious to those watching. In a world full of broken homes and broken marriages, people want to see real, concrete love. When they see it in dance, they want to know the God who makes it possible.

Obviously not everyone will be touched by such a demonstration. Dancing is not to everyone's taste and therefore there are many for whom performed dance is mystifying or ridiculous. It is totally outside their experience and perhaps the only dance they know is the suggestive disco dancing on television. I'm under no illusions. I have to look to God to speak to them in some other way. Having said this, however, I cannot deny the striking effect dance has had on the most unlikely types.

Once I danced with another girl to the song quoted above, 'Come, Lord Jesus', in Belfast's Cromlyn Road gaol. I was with a team who went in with David Watson to give a talk. They were political prisoners and hardened criminals—and they hadn't exactly chosen to come to the service.

If we'd had any sense, we would have omitted the dance on this occasion. Fortunately we hadn't, although there

was a strong temptation to hide all the girls in the back
row of the singing group. We had decided to do a dance,
though, and so we did.

As Sue and I got up and took our places to begin, we
fully expected jeers and whistles to continue throughout
the song, just because we were two women in front of a
hall full of men. As soon as the song started, however, and
we began to move, a hush seemed to descend on the
gathering. It was so unexpected. The rustling and nudging
and coughing and whispering seemed to cease—or
certainly dropped right down.

There was no jeering or clapping at the end, just silence.
Whether stunned or reverential, I'm not sure. But David
rose to speak into that silence. He spoke very clearly and
simply to those prisoners, many of whom were convicted
terrorists, whose lives were practically built on sectarian
hatred, and he spoke about the reconciliation Jesus died
to give us. Men came to Christ as a result of that meeting,
and forgiveness replaced bitterness in several hearts.

A group ministry

The ministry of dance is a group ministry, for if the dance
is to have any meaning at all it must come out of our life
together. The group working together both 'on stage' and
'off', reflects the whole body of Christ worshipping together, living together, and reaching out to the world
together. In the next chapter I shall talk in much more
detail about this.

How do I know the Lord is calling me to a dance ministry?

You would not believe how many times I have been asked
over the last ten years: 'How do I know whether or not I
have been called into the ministry of dance?' It is amazing
how illogical we can be when discerning whether or not

we have a gift of dance. It is in fact no different from being called, for example, to a preaching ministry. Initially, a preacher may have little or no idea that he has a particular gift in this area. He has a vision for it, certainly, and a love for it. Then others begin to tell him that the Lord is blessing his preaching, and he realizes that perhaps he must take it more seriously. He studies hard and works at it, maybe even taking voice lessons from a drama teacher, and as he works at it, the Lord anoints him with an effectiveness that goes beyond human endeavour.

As with any ministry, knowing whether or not you are a good dancer is not usually sufficient to discern whether or not you are being led into a dance ministry. The most important thing is that you should have a vision for how God can use it, both in the life of the individual and in the life of the church. Also, you must have a love for it! You are probably saying to yourself, 'Yes, I do have a vision for it, and I love it, but I've no ability whatsoever. I've certainly never done any training.' If so, then you are like 90% of all other people involved in a dance ministry, including me!

I had no idea that I could dance. The first person in our church to have a vision and a gift and a ministry was Kay Taylor. She began the dance group, and I joined it because I had been so inspired by the visit of 'Shekinah' that I described earlier.

In fact, it was during their visit that I first tried dancing for the Lord. It was a Festival of Praise in York Minster and the sense of the Lord's presence was very, very real. I felt so close to Jesus, and so thrilled by him, that it seemed the most natural thing in the world to kick off my shoes and duck under the two or three people between me and the aisle. Who knows what other people thought! Fortunately I was sitting near the back. The darkness in that part of the cathedral gave me courage, and I danced for the Lord!

After that I began to go to the weekly dance-drama meeting that Kay was leading. A year later the church was visited by some members of the Fisherfolk from the Post Green Christian community. They led a week of workshops in dance, drama and music, and at the end of this week it was suggested that I should take more of a leadership role in the York dance group.

That surprised no one more than me. Yet I have always been grateful to the Lord for the way he has led me step by step, because his direction has nearly always come through the encouragement of other people. So often when I have automatically thought that I wouldn't be doing any more dancing (for example, after the birth of each of our three children) God has opened up new doors for me.

When I thought I would never have to touch my toes again, let alone do a proper *plié*, I have had to ask God to give me the ability to dance again, and to do some hard work as well.

I want to encourage those of you who have a vision for dance and who love it, but don't think you have the ability. If God is leading you into the ministry, then he will give you the gift. He has done it with me and he will do it with you.

Certainly there are trained and professional dancers who serve the Lord full time with their gift, and there are already a handful of full-time Christian dance groups in this country. Sometimes I look at these people with longing, and wonder why I never had the opportunity to do years of dance training. However, the testimony of professional dancers is often that their training has *hindered* their ministry. Sometimes they have found it difficult to allow the Holy Spirit to work freely through their dance. Sometimes their own ability to worship God through movement is held down by their dance technique.

Working it out

But before you all settle back comfortably in your chairs with the thought that you don't need to do any work because the Lord is going to give you the gift, and anyway, training would *hinder* your dancing, remember the preacher. He knows that he must honour God in the gift that he is being given, and therefore he must study and work at it too. If you were part of the music ministry of your church, you would never dream of playing your instrument without practice and application.

So, if you are being called into a dance ministry, you must take it seriously and be committed to it as a calling from God. You must be prepared to be committed to the meetings or services of your fellowship for you know that at any time the Holy Spirit might call you out to minister in dance; committed also to the rest of the dance group, and to seeking the Lord week by week with them to discern his will for each service; committed to leading your church into all that God has for them in the area of dance, both personal and corporate; committed to worshipping God, and to spreading his word.

This means that even if you have not choreographed or planned a dance for a particular service, you must go to that service prepared to dance. Commitment isn't easy. It isn't always easy to think, 'Am I OK wearing this if the Lord calls me to dance?' and, as you enter the church, 'I must sit where I can easily move out if necessary.'

It is also very important to train your body to dance. Unfortunately there is a tendency for Christians to regard a professional attitude towards something as somehow unspiritual—'We mustn't become too professional, or we won't relate to the man in the pew', etc. In fact, the work of a dancer is to direct people's eyes to the Lord, and this is hindered if he or she is self-conscious because of having to concentrate on the dance itself and not on God. The

more you train, the more you will be able to dance with
freedom, and the less those watching will notice you as an
individual.

Try to attend a dance class at least once a week. New
ones are being started almost weekly in every town and
city, so you shouldn't have too much difficulty in finding
one, perhaps through your local education authority. If
you are a beginner, then contemporary is best, although if
you can find a beginners' ballet class for adults, much can
be learnt from the discipline. Keep-fit classes are all right
if there is nothing else available, for obviously the more
you build up your fitness and strength, the greater control
you will have in your dancing.

The ups and downs

The 'ups' of having a ministry of dance for the Lord are
immeasurable. It is such a privilege to be called by God to
worship him in this way, and to be given the opportunity
to encourage others to do so too.

But because of the very nature of the ministry, an
openness and a vulnerability are required that sometimes
result in being hurt. 'Through dance I have learned to love
more, but being open to love has meant being open to
pain too', a girl said to me once. If people have resentments and bitternesses, they often use the dance and the
dancers as a scapegoat for their feelings.

Let me give you an example to explain this more clearly.

There was a girl in our church some years ago who was
very, very angry with God that she wasn't married. Partly
because of this, she believed that she wasn't attractive,
either physically or in her personality, and as a Christian
she believed she was second rate. She worked in close
contact with some of the girls who were in the dance
group, but whenever dance came up in conversation, she
would walk out of the room. Eventually, she became so

cold towards the dancers she would hardly talk to them, and turned away with hatred in her eyes. The situation grew steadily worse until it seemed that the whole of her being was focused on one thing—tearing down the dance group.

It was very distressing, because we couldn't understand why she hated us so much. Some months later we learnt from a lady who had spent much time counselling her, that healing in this girl's life had started when she had begun to hate the dance group. There were so many things in her life about which she was bitter and resentful, but because she felt guilty about these feelings she had repressed them. In order to be healed of these things, the wound needed to be opened and cleansed. Because we in the dance group seemed to represent for her everything she thought she wasn't (attractive, spiritual, etc.) she directed her pent-up anger at us. Painful for us, but at last there was something in her life that was opened up enough for the Lord to begin to heal.

Similar, though less traumatic incidents have happened over and over again. Those of us in the dance ministry need to pray for humility, grace and love. We need to reaffirm daily in our hearts that we are nothing without God. Everything that we are, everything that we do is by grace and grace alone. We are just empty vessels ready to be used by God.

Some years ago I danced during a fellowship praise and prayer meeting. As I sat down, an old lady muttered in a voice the whole room could hear, 'ridiculous, ridiculous'. I was devastated, but as I looked up I caught the eye of the leader of the meeting. I knew immediately from his face that he thought that what I had done had been completely of the Lord, and that he was giving me his covering.

To move out into the ministry of dance you need to know you have the covering of the leader or leaders of your church. Even if you make a huge mistake, and dance at completely the wrong time, you are not on your own. There is someone else to help shoulder the blame, and to show us that in the end God covers our mistakes. Such covering is not automatically available. That is why it is important to pray together often and think through the issues with the church leader who would take this role over you in the ministry of dance.

In the Spirit

When is it right to dance, and when is it not? What is the difference between a dance that is prepared for the service a week in advance, and a dance that is spontaneous? Unfortunately the phrase 'dancing in the Spirit' is used by some people to refer only to spontaneous dancing. This implies that a carefully planned and choreographed dance is not 'in the Spirit'.

In the same way that the preacher prayerfully prepares his talk, most dances are choreographed in advance, knowing that the Holy Spirit is well able to give a dance that is going to be appropriate for the worship to come.

Some churches have a 'worship committee'. This is often composed of, for example, the clergy, the leader of the dance group, the musical director, and sometimes the leaders of the banner-making group, and they will meet together once a week to plan the coming services. As this small group seeks the Lord together, he shows what is *his* will for each part of the 'tapestry' that is corporate worship.

Spontaneous worship, on the other hand, is not usually choreographed. If you have a ministry of dance, you must ask the Lord at the beginning of each service to show you if he wants you to move out in dance. Learning to be sensitive to God takes time and practice. If you think it is right to dance, ask the Lord to confirm it to you. Even if he seems to, you must be prepared to make mistakes. Once or twice I have left the pew and moved out into the front of the church, only to realize that I have misheard the Lord. One or two quick twirls and I creep back to my place, praying that no one has noticed me! When it has been right, though, at least one person has told me afterwards how the dance has ministered to them.

Sometimes I really *feel* like dancing. Sometimes it is just a matter of obedience. I know that I am unworthy to praise God in this way, but Jesus has paid the price of my sin, and it is in his robe of righteousness that I dance. Sometimes I am terribly aware of my own fallen nature, especially in the area of wrong motives. All I can do is ask God to cleanse me, and to use me none the less. Those of us in a dance ministry should always pray before we dance that those watching might not notice us as individuals, but see only the Lord.

Finally, a sense of humour helps! Sue Hope is a dear friend and sister in Christ, and we have danced together for years. On one occasion we both leapt out during the magnificent final hymn of a particularly glorious and uplifting service. Everything was fine until Sue mistimed a spin, lost her balance, and fell flat on her face, right in front of the vicar and all the elders! She wasn't hurt, but she looked so ridiculous that everyone at the front burst out laughing, including Sue. Such is the glory of God that everyone's shared joke only added to the final celebration of that evening service.

9. *The Dance Group*

In practice, the ministry of dance is most often worked out in the dance group or dance choir. If you have been called to dance full time for the Lord, or if you work with a travelling team who visit churches around the country to bring renewal, your dance group may be no more than two or three in number. Possibly you act and sing as well.

On the other hand, there may be as many as fifteen of you who are meeting to explore dance in worship. You may all be single, and able to meet four times a week, or you may all be married with small children, and only able to manage twice a month. We worry far too much about trying to conform to the same pattern as 'the church next door' and yet God has a different work to do in every local church situation, and we must learn to listen to his leadings.

When we began to dance in York ten years ago, if there were other local church dance groups in the country we didn't know of them, and so we had to rely on God's leadings as each step was taken. The Lord spoke to us in many ways, often through words of prophecy, and he confirmed to us again and again that it was *his* work that we were doing.

Of course there were also plenty of problems. But, as always, God's hand was in the problems too, because many of us have gone on to share around the country what we learnt in those first few years.

This chapter is about group ministry, and the working out of a group ministry is the same whether you are singers, dancers, actors or evangelists, so some of this chapter may seem to be obvious. Nevertheless, sometimes even the obvious needs to be repeated!

The composition of the dance group

Very often a group begins to come together because the leaders of a church want to use dance in a particular service. So they ask someone who they feel has possibly the same vision, and a gift of leadership, to call together others who are like-minded to work on a dance for this specific occasion.

If you are one of these church leaders, then a word of warning. Please don't assume that just because there is someone in your congregation who is a trained dancer that she should lead a dance group, or in fact that she is necessarily being called into a ministry of dance. All too often the dance ministry in a church starts off on a poor footing (sorry!) because the wrong leader is chosen.

There are so many things that matter more than an immediate ability to dance. A very deep love of the Lord—a desire to worship him come what may—is necessary beyond all things. The leader needs to be willing to lay down her life for the rest of the group, as well as for the whole church. Because dance is so often such a sensitive subject, she needs to be gentle and diplomatic, yet firm when problems arise.

If such a person also has a vision for dance, then not only will she be able to lead others in a ministry, but what is in her heart will give her own dancing freedom and grace that will minister to others.

Should there be men in the group? Could the leader of the group be a man? It would be wonderful if there could be more men in the dance ministry, but as this is still very rare, I am assuming that I am writing here mostly for women. In time, perhaps God will draw more men into this work, but before then we need to learn much more as a church about freedom and acceptance.

I know of many men who find dance the most natural way to worship God. Also I know one or two who undoubtedly have a dance ministry. When they use their gift the Lord uses them very, very powerfully. The reaction of the rest of the body of Christ has always been very positive too, and many have said (both men and women) how the dance has touched them. I believe the dance ministry will only come into its full potential when men and women take an equal part in it.

There are two ways of discovering those in a church with a possible dance ministry. One is simply to pray that those who are like-minded will make themselves known to one another. The other is to hold a series of seminars or workshops open to the whole church, and then work with those who persevere as the meetings continue. There are pros and cons for both.

In the first instance, I am sure that there are many people who are excluded from the dance ministry because they never have the opportunity to learn about dancing for the Lord. If the first dancing they see is that of a small established group in the church, it never occurs to them that this might be something to which God is calling them.

On the other hand, one difficulty with holding open workshops, and calling that the dance group, is that there will inevitably be some who sincerely believe they are being given a ministry when sadly they are not.

Nevertheless, the second pattern is probably better. If at all possible, invite someone from outside the church who already has an established dance ministry to come and teach and to lead these early workshops. Such a person will have the ability to discern a gift of dance in others, and will be able to advise on the initial direction of the group. If it isn't possible to bring in anyone from outside, then there are some suggestions for such a workshop at the end of this chapter.

Why is the composition of the group so difficult? Why is it that bringing together those with a dance ministry seems to be more of a problem than bringing together, say, the singing group? The reason is that to be told that you can't dance is for many people much more difficult to accept than to be told you can't sing. This is why the leader needs to be gentle but firm, and why she needs to know that she has the authority given to her by God through the leaders of the church.

A very helpful guideline is that no one should be allowed actually to minister in dance, in church, until they have been a member of the group for some months. During this time the leader or leaders will be able to discern whether or not the newcomer has the 'gift of dance'. But how *do* you know that someone is right to dance? Certainly, the *ability* to dance takes time to develop. Surely if someone's heart is 'in the right place', nothing else matters?

The leader of the group needs to ask the Lord to help her discern whether or not someone's desire to dance in public is a God-given desire that he will use. Very often the answer will come in the way the newcomer harmonizes with the rest of the group. A group may be full of people of all shapes and sizes, ages and abilities, and yet when they dance together, no one individual should stand out among the rest.

If at the end of a service, members of the congregation remark to the leader of the group that one dancer is always slightly behind the others, then something is wrong. Unfortunately, the reason may be that she is plumper and a little older than the others and finds it difficult to keep up. If this continues, it may be necessary to keep this person from dancing in church for a time to consider more carefully their calling to this ministry.

It may be that in time God will bring into the group others who are exactly right to dance with the 'odd one out'. The leader must realize, however, that this person may be out of step for reasons other than physical ability or stature. Then, however painful it is, she may have to be asked to step down from dancing in public.

The ministry of the group as a whole is more important than the hurt feelings of one individual. A ministry must be glorifying to God and edifying to the whole body of Christ. When the dance group is in such harmony that it is seen as a whole, then the attention of those watching will be directed towards God, and away from the group and from the individuals who are taking part.

'Telling the truth in love' is not easy in situations like this, but it is one of the ways to deeper and more caring relationships in the body of Christ. We are afraid to be cruel because we do not trust our own motives, but we should not shy away from confrontation that may result in deep healing and a new harmony.

When and where to meet, and in what?

The answer to 'when?' is not only 'regularly'. It is also 'every time a meeting is held'. In other words, if you decide to meet once a week, or once a month, then each member must realize that this meeting must take top priority. It is not something you attend just when you feel like it.

If you have small children and a husband, then in effect the whole family must be committed to the dance ministry. Going out one evening a week is not too bad, but when it comes to leaving three screaming children and a distraught husband at 4.30 p.m. on a Sunday afternoon in order to rehearse before a Sunday evening service, then you have to know that your husband believes in what you are doing.

It does seem that when God draws a dance group together, those who become members are able to give a similar commitment of time. For example, when we began in York we were all single, and able to meet three evenings a week. I met a group from Leeds some time ago who were all married with school-age children. Obviously, the best time for them to meet was during the day.

The answer to 'where?' is not necessarily the church hall. Warmth is nearly as important as space for a congenial atmosphere in which to put together a dance, and church halls, I hardly need to point out, are not always warm. Have a hunt round your area. Look for a floor congenial to bare feet, warmth, space and, ideally, facilities for making hot drinks (vital to group dynamics).

You should wear proper dance gear if at all possible when you meet. A pianist cannot rehearse wearing gloves and a preacher wouldn't dream of preparing sermons without a good Bible commentary to hand. If you are a dancer you need a leotard and footless tights and lots of warm layers to pile on top. Leg warmers may have become a fashion accessory, but for dance they are in fact very practical. Muscles work much better if they are kept warm. If you are prone to foot cramp, as I am, wear thick socks for warming up. They will make all the difference. Apart from anything else, if you dress like a dancer, you may feel a bit more like a dancer—and anything helps!

Sharing your life

Unless the individuals in the group are prepared to open up to one another, the dancing will be lifeless, and may even show discord and disharmony. Relationships are central and the dance group should be a place where the principles of a shared life can be worked out on a very practical level; where we can learn what it means to be part of the body of Christ:

> Rather, speaking the truth in love, we are to grow up in every way into him who is the head, into Christ, from whom the whole body joined and knit together by every joint with which it is supplied, when each part is working properly, makes bodily growth and upbuilds itself in love (Eph 4:15–16, RSV).

I am very grateful for that chapter in the history of our group when several of us not only danced together, but also lived together and worked together every day. It was a very intense time, certainly, and I am not suggesting it as a pattern for all. But our experience was that as we allowed the Lord to build up love and trust among us— through the pain of fears and misunderstandings—the dance became a powerful witness to the life of unity and of love to which he was calling the whole church.

Each week, at the beginning of your meeting, share

with one another what is going on in your lives spiritually, as well as your problems at work and in your homes. A dance group needs to learn to pray for one another and to ask God for the spiritual gifts within the group, that through them God might build up and strengthen the members.

Of course, relationships are not just worked out in this one hour, but throughout the whole of the meeting. As we learn to accept one another as Christ accepts us, instead of being critical and judgemental, we will find that different members of the group have different things to give.

As we submit to one another in order to serve both the group and the church, personal sacrifice is inevitably involved. We must always be willing to learn, however skilled we may be in a particular area.

Individuals who are secure in their relationship in a group will be in an environment where they can develop spiritually, as well as in their creative gifts. God's provision for our healing and growth is his body working properly. A willingness to learn from the Lord through one another will be costly but healing, and it will bring us into the fullness of life that God intends for each of us.

Worshipping together

The first calling of the dance group is to worship the Lord. God loves to be worshipped on a Tuesday evening in the church hall, just as much as on a Sunday in church. Being able to worship freely and openly together on a Sunday evening only comes after learning to dance freely for the Lord with one another in the group, and at such times the group not only learns to praise together, but also to receive what the Lord is saying. Commitment to worship, prayer and meditation may mean that we do not dance in every service, but the dances will soon become empty shells if not based on the reality of corporate worship.

Dances for professional companies are usually choreographed by a single person, and if you have available someone with that kind of experience, you will of course want to use them. When the whole group works together on a dance, however, the give and take of ideas can result in a close unity, which in turn becomes part of the powerful ministry of the dance when it is performed.

Begin of course by asking the Lord to help you use the time. He knows what you have to do, and how little time you have to do it in.

Next do a work-out (see the section entitled 'Make It Work'). It is dishonouring to the gift God has given you and to the ministry to which you are called if you neglect the discipline and training of your body. Furthermore, there is danger of injury if you are trying unfamiliar movements and have not warmed and stretched your muscles first.

Having done that, you may be acutely aware of the limitations of your bodies. This is the time to press on with confidence. You may not be trained dancers, but you can still give your best. Whatever your skill, much beauty, life and grace can be seen in very simple movements done well. Working within your limits physically can often reveal and convey a much greater inner freedom in worship than striving to achieve a dramatic performance and not quite making it: 'If you can't land, don't jump.'

Now listen to the song, the hymn or the music you have chosen and pray again that the Holy Spirit will guide you to the dance that is just right for the service and setting where it is to be performed.

As you play back the piece three or four times, begin to move to it individually. You will soon discover as you share your ideas that a definite pattern is emerging. The work of the leader is very important because she needs to know when to say yes to an idea, and when to say no. If she is unsure of her own ability in this direction, she needs to know who to look to in the group for a final word.

It is exciting to see different gifts dovetailing together in a group to form a whole, and it is important for the leader to draw out these gifts. After listening to the song or music, one person may immediately go to her Bible in order to share a verse that she believes will help to clarify the direction of the dance. Another may sense what shapes the dance should make, and someone else will know how to interpret these individual ideas in specific movements.

A mistake that is easily made is the assumption that every dancer should be used for every dance. The best number is four or five and always have one person 'standing in the wings' to advise as the dance is rehearsed.

Obviously, the more rehearsal time you can put in, the better. God can use a dance that has been put together in a hurry with little rehearsal, if that is all you can manage. But it is very sad that we can be perfectionists in the superficial things of life, and yet are prepared to offer second-best to God's work: 'Is it a time for you yourselves to be living in your panelled houses, while this house [the temple] lies in ruins?' (Hag 1:4, RSV).

If the part of his house that the Lord has given you to work on is dance, then you neglect it at your peril. It may take hours of commitment and hard work, but God will bless you and others through it.

As the group spends more and more time together it will learn to listen to the Holy Spirit. The creation of a new dance is *his* work because he knows how the dance is going to minister to others when it is performed. This is why it is that only occasionally one group will be able to teach one of their dances to another group.

If you meet on the same evening as the singing group and the drama group, and they all go off home at 9.30 p.m. while you have to slog on until 11 p.m., be encouraged that it is the same for every local church dance ministry throughout the country. God is using dance powerfully throughout his church, and this requires sacrifice and hard work on the part of the dancers.

What to wear for the service

If you are surprised that I am devoting a section of this chapter to 'what to wear' then you haven't had much experience of a local church dance group! Just as everybody is about to go home to their beds, someone remembers: 'Well, folks, what are we going to wear on Sunday?'—and you all sit down again for a thirty-minute discussion. So here are some helpful hints.

Before you all go out and spend money on new clothes, make do with what you already have. A style will probably emerge that will suit you all, and it is too costly to make mistakes in the beginning. It is worth taking a whole evening experimenting with shapes, colours and styles.

What you are looking for are clothes that will blend together. Either a common style in different colours, or different styles in the same colour. There are, though, two rules. All skirts must be the same length. And tops must *not* be tight! To my mind, therefore, leotards with wrapover skirts may be all right for rehearsing, but they are not at all suitable for church dance.

Choose colours that are right for different occasions. 'Jewel' colours for Christmas, red, gold and yellow for harvest festival. If you need to buy something new, then choose a white or cream blouse with three-quarters-length sleeves for everybody. These can be worn with different cotton skirts, or pinafore dresses. If your church is cold in winter, thermal underwear is the answer! In time, a style that suits everyone will emerge, and then the group can go ahead with making or buying a standard dance dress.

Men should aim for something that is simple and easy to move in. Stretch canvas trousers in black or grey are ideal, with a solid colour long-sleeved shirt, or a T-shirt.

A final word

The first calling of the dance group is to worship God, and as you offer praise and worship to him, he can use you as a group to minister to his people.

The value of the dance group in the church lies in its artistic and worshipful expression of the life of Christ in us and among us. Its validity comes from the truth and reality of that life, not only in the group itself, but in the corporate life of the whole church.

As you open up to others in trust and in love, you are vulnerable. You may be hurt, and you may hurt others. You may lose some inhibitions. But you may also find yourself rejoicing in the healing and the fruitfulness in dance that the Lord gives:

> For the Lord takes delight in his people; he crowns the humble with salvation (Ps 149:4, RSV).

Appendix: Leading Workshops

One of the most important parts of the ministry of the dance group is to teach the members of the church about the importance of dance in the life of every individual. It will also be the dance group who will initiate and lead congregational dance, and it is by holding workshops that those things can happen.

Workshops are not designed to produce finished pieces in the space of one afternoon. To ask someone who has never used any movement at all in his relationship with God immediately to dance in public leads only to confusion and misunderstanding. The first aim of a dance workshop is not to pass on a few movements, but to lead everyone who is there into a deeper relationship with God. If in the two hours available it is only possible to help people gain one new insight into God's wonderful love for them and to have a further understanding of how acceptable they are in God's sight, then in fact a great deal has been achieved.

Obviously, then, one workshop on its own is not enough, and the dance group should try and hold a series of three or four. Here are a few ideas and guidelines.

Begin the meeting by teaching a very simple Israeli dance to everyone. This immediately releases people and encourages fellowship and openness at the start. While people are regaining their breath explain the structure of the workshop or workshops, and especially explain the aims. Ask each person in turn why they have come and what experience they already have in dance; this is very reassuring for everyone and it is absolutely necessary for the leader to know how much understanding of dance people already have.

A helpful structure for three workshops is:

1. private dance;
2. corporate dance;
3. public dance.

Base the first one on Psalm 40: 3a—'He put a new song in my mouth, a hymn of praise to our God' (NIV). The aim is to encourage each individual in a new love for the Lord, as well as a new acceptance and understanding of his love for them. At the beginning, help people to focus their minds not on dance, themselves or each other, but on to the Lord.

Meditate together for a short while on a verse, preferably one that speaks of God's amazing, complete, unquestioning love for us as individuals, e.g. Jn 3:16— 'For God so loved the world that he gave his one and only Son, that whoever believes in him shall not perish but have eternal life' (NIV). Lead from the meditation into a short time of worship, and gently encourage people to raise their arms, to kneel or to walk round the room if they want to. Sometimes the Holy Spirit moves very powerfully and this time of worship becomes exciting, releasing people right at the beginning into a new freedom and self-acceptance.

At other times the leader will realize that much careful biblical teaching needs to be given about God's longing that we should come to him as whole people, and that there is nothing that God wants more than our praise, however much it costs us. Meditate on verses in the Bible that show that our bodies are not unfortunate extras but part of that humanity with which we are to glorify God, e.g. 1 Cor 6:13—'The body is not meant for sexual immorality, but for the Lord, and the Lord for the body' (NIV).

One way of helping people to accept their bodies is to meditate on verses in the Bible that mention different parts of the body. Here is a list of ideas:

1. *The body.* Genesis 2:7 (NIV): 'And the Lord God formed man from the dust of the ground and breathed into his nostrils the breath of life, and man became a living being' (also Ps 139:13–14).

2. *The face.* Exodus 34:29—When Moses came down from the mountain after receiving the Ten Commandments from God, '. . . the skin of his face shone because he had been talking with God'.

3. *The head.* Psalm 27:6 (NIV): 'Then my head will be exalted above the enemies who surround me.'

4. *Hair.* Luke 12:7: Jesus said that even the hairs of our head are numbered.'

5. *Ear and eye.* Proverbs 20:12 (NIV): 'Ears that hear and eyes that see—the Lord has made them both.'

6. *Tongue/mouth.* James 3:9 (NIV): 'With the tongue we praise our Lord and Father, and with it we curse men, who have been made in God's likeness.'

7. *Lips. Psalm 63:3 (*NIV): 'Because your love is better than life, my lips will glorify you.'

8. *Hands.* Luke 24:50 (RSV): 'Then he led them out as far as Bethany, and lifting up his hands he blessed them.'

9. *Feet.* Psalm 119:105 (NIV): 'Your Word is a lamp to my feet and a light for my path.'

The aim for the end of this first workshop is to spend as much time as possible helping each individual to begin personally to worship God in dance. The leader needs to be aware of the needs and problems of each person there. It is particularly wonderful when the Lord leads the members of a group to minister and pray for one another. As people begin to try and dance for the Lord they may discover many things about themselves that they were not aware of, and as healing takes place, God can change lives.

The second workshop could be based on Ephesians 4:15 and 16:

> Rather, speaking the truth in love, we are to grow up in every way into him who is the head, into Christ, from whom the whole body, joined and knit together by every joint with which it is supplied, when each part is working properly, makes bodily growth and upbuilds itself in love (RSV).

The aim of this session is to help people discover how dance can bring us into a new love and service to each other. As before, begin by centring people's minds on the Lord with meditation and a time of worship. Perhaps teach some simple movements to help people become more and more free in dance. Encourage them to begin to look at one another dancing, to accept that not only does God love us, but that we must accept the love of one another.

The leader may feel it is time now to begin to create a dance, using the same principles that are used each week in the dance group. This can be very exciting as people begin to discover the joys of sharing in this way.

The final workshop could be based on Psalm 40:3b— 'Many will see and fear and put their trust in the Lord.' The aim here is to show people how a new love for the Lord and a new love for one another results in others being ministered to, both Christians and non-Christians. Think of the witness to the world today that there is in joyous dance. What would it be like for someone encountering this on the street in front of your church or walking into your church and finding dancing in the aisles along with the heartfelt singing?

This final workshop may also be the place to challenge people even further to have a deep love for the Lord, and to know what he has for us. If so, turn together to parts of the Song of Songs, and wait for him to speak to your heart.

In all the workshops, make every effort to help people to relax and to assure them that whatever they offer to God with a pure heart will be acceptable to him.

Don't forget, too, some simple warm-up and stretching exercises before attempting unfamiliar movements with those who may never have used their bodies expressively.

Finally, be sure to use all our more usual forms of worship—prayer, intercession, singing and studying Scripture—to put dance into a right perspective: one way among many that we have to proclaim that Jesus Christ is Lord of lords, and King of kings.

STEPS OF FAITH

We live in an age where the image very often speaks louder than the word.

Geoffrey Stevenson has delighted thousands with his poignant and unforgettable mimes, highlighting God's unchanging truth and leaving us with impressions that stay in our minds long afterwards.

His wife Judith is one of the pioneers of dance in worship, and both she and Geoffrey have worked on missions of evangelism and renewal. Here for the first time are practical guidelines for dance and drama groups who wish to learn the techniques that will add new dimensions to their worship and outreach.

The book is divided into three parts, with the Mime and Dance sections beginning from either end, both illustrated with line drawings. In the middle is a section for both mime artists and dancers, to help them limber up and keep in shape.

Steps
of
Faith

A Practical Introduction to
Mime and Dance

GEOFFREY & JUDITH STEVENSON

KINGSWAY PUBLICATIONS
EASTBOURNE

ISBN 0 86065 275 0

Front cover photo (mime): Claire Oliver
Front cover photo (dance): John G. Stevenson

Illustrations (mime) by Vic Mitchell
Illustrations (dance) by Janet Lunt

Printed in Great Britain for
KINGSWAY PUBLICATIONS LTD
Lottbridge Drove, Eastbourne, E. Sussex BN23 6NT by
Richard Clay (The Chaucer Press) Ltd, Bungay, Suffolk.
Typeset by Nuprint Services Ltd, Harpenden, Herts.

Contents

Acknowledgements   6
Foreword by Anne Watson   7
Introduction   9

MIME

1. What Is Mime?   14
2. Mime in the Church   19
3. Holding the Stage   32
4. Basic Mime   41
5. Character   49
6. Illusions   57
7. Creating Your Own Work   67
   Appendix: Notes on Performing Mime, and Two Pieces   72

MAKE IT WORK   87

Bibliography   104

DANCE

1. What Is Dance—Sacred, Secular or Silly?   8
2. The Challenge to Christians:
   Why We Should Dance   23
3. So Why Don't We Dance?   38
4. Worship   47
5. Try It, Try It, You Will See . . .   53
6. Keep Going—There Is More to Explore!   63
7. Congregational Dance   75
8. Dance Ministry   87
9. The Dance Group   101
   Appendix: Leading workshops   113

Acknowledgements

Our thanks go to Liz Rowland and Liz and Alistair Mack for proof-reading, editing and constant encouragement; to both our mothers, for continuing to love us in such practical and sacrifical ways, and particularly for caring for our children; and of course to our children themselves, Elizabeth, Anna, and Geoffrey John, without whom all this would have been much more feasible!

Foreword

Originally David, my husband, was to have written this foreword. I know from what he had read of this book that he was very excited about it.

David and I met Judith when we visited her parents' home for dinner one evening. Judith and I discovered we had a common link—we were both Guy's nurses. The link was strengthened later when she gave me such wonderful help with a large fourteen-room Rectory and a small four-year-old daughter. However, it was not until we both joined the dance group at St Michael-le-Belfrey, York, that our friendship really developed. I admired her for the beautiful way she was able to move her body; her whole being seemed to be expressed as she danced. Her love for God was obviously a deep motivating factor in her life, and when this was combined with clear vision, creative movement and a gentle, joyful spirit, many people were encouraged to take steps of faith. The dance group blossomed under her leadership and I know that David valued her support, as well as her creative gifts while she was a member of his travelling team.

Geoffrey arrived to live in our extended household while we were having tea one afternoon. He introduced us to the phenomena of peanut butter and jelly (jam) sandwiches! He was a marvellous cook and we all hung around the kitchen when he was busy there. His preparation was a joy to watch—an artist at work. Our gastric juices anticipating something delicious, we were never disappointed; even scrambled eggs were 'out of this world'! Geoffrey had a great gift for bringing the other side of the story to light in sometimes heated household debates. With his quiet smile and real wisdom, he spoke with his whole body and we all listened and relaxed!

Encouraging him to take up mime as a full time occupation was something David and I did wholeheartedly. Geoffrey had been a member of the travelling team and during that time David had seen his faith and hard work in action. The steps of faith he later took have been used by God to be a blessing to many people. At last we can read just what those steps were, and I trust begin to go forward and appropriate them ourselves. A whole new way of speaking to people anaesthetized by words is within our grasp. Let us begin now to move out with faith.

What Geoffrey and Judith share in this book can be compared to the unveiling of another lovely expression of the creativity of God. Faith and hard work will be required so that it can be reproduced in churches and fellowships, not only in this country but far beyond. May the Holy Spirit find many who will be willing to take those steps of faith.

Anne Watson
London

1. *Introduction*

'The dance is the child of music. Pantomime is the child of silence. But, though they come from opposite poles, the dancer and the mime are running to meet each other.' The writer of this quotation was Jean-Louis Barrault, the famous French actor, director and mime artist. He was speaking metaphorically, of course, for there is indeed a great gulf between the art of mime and the whole medium of dance. But perhaps we would agree with Barrault that in some ways this gulf has been narrowing in recent times.

In a strange way, however, the quote aptly describes the basis for this book. We are a happily married couple involved in two quite different art forms. Perhaps as the distinctions are increasingly blurred we will become even more happily married! Later on, we will define both mime and dance. But for the moment we will just say that there is enough of a bodily connection between them to justify treating the two subjects together.

Certainly the public, inside and outside of the church, are receiving the arts with greater awareness and sophistication, and with fewer rigidly defined expectations and preconceptions. More significantly, this book arises from a belief that God is bringing, along with spiritual renewal and the stirrings of revival, a certain 'flowering' of the arts of all kinds in his church.

9

This flowering should not be dismissed as something superficial and superfluous to the real work of 'the kingdom'. Life—in particular the fullness of life that is ours through Jesus—is too rich and varied for that. The God we (imperfectly) reflect in our lives, as we are perfected and changed by him 'from one degree of glory to another', is a Creator God of beauty and majesty as well as compassion and holiness, mercy and justice.

Our chosen disciplines are of course dear to our hearts, and it is natural to write about such things with feeling. But they are *only* two of the wide range of art forms that God is at present redeeming from the world's misuse and misappropriation.

Nor is the irony lost on us of a book of words about two supremely non-verbal methods of communication. Alexander Pope's verse

> True ease in writing comes from art, not chance,
> As those move easiest who have learn'd to dance

must give us all pause for thought! However, we press on, although it is even difficult to find good quotations on the subject of communication without words.

Swinburne's 'For words divide and rend; But silence is most noble till the end' gives some comfort, but most inspiring perhaps is St Jerome: 'I have revered always not crude verbosity, but holy simplicity'.

In the end we can only think of Shakespeare's 'men of few words are the best men'. We are trying to be true to that in dance and mime, and writing too—with rather less success!

What this book is not

It is not:

> a contribution to an academic theology of worship;
> a book of choreographed dances and set mime pieces;
> a Bible study on 'I harden my body with blows, and
> bring it under complete control' (1 Cor 9:27, GNB);
> a historical survey;
> unbiased;
> the latest fad;
> the last word.

What the book is

Instead, it is a work, according to our respective experiences
and interest in mime and dance, in two rather different
parts. One section of the book is on the subject of dance in
worship, personal and corporate, from many angles. The
section that starts at the other end of the book is about
mime. In between is a section on our most obvious
common ground, that of limbering up our bodies. This is
entitled 'Make It Work'. There is theory, inspiration (we
hope) and practical work in all three parts. Finally, a
bibliography is included, and as there is no 'back of the
book' (!), this comes at the end of 'Make It Work'.

Whichever way your interest lies, we urge you to delve
deeply into *all* the book, not just your area of prime
interest. They are, we believe, complementary aspects of
an understanding that is growing in, or perhaps returning
to, the church today. This is an understanding of how our
bodies, indeed our whole selves, can be used in our walk
with God and in our communication with others of the
knowledge and love of God in our lives.

We would like to say how they *should* be used, but we
believe there are enough personal opinions and possibly

contentious statements in the book already. So if you differ on any, or many, points, please forgive us for our wrong thinking. And please understand, dear reader, that although our opinions happen to be in print, it does not mean that you could not, with grace, persuade us differently.

There are undoubtedly those reading this book who will fundamentally disagree with us. Perhaps your understanding of God and his ways is or seems a trifle different to ours.

Perhaps you do not 'know' God at all.

In the first instance it is our greatest desire that such differences will not separate you from us as brothers and sisters in Christ, but that together we will grow to understand more perfectly the things of God.

In the second instance, we hope and pray that in these pages, you who do not share our faith will find a glimmer of the reality of Jesus, who is alive and well and living in his church. It is out of love for, and obedience to, him that we are engaged in mime and dance in the church.

We owe, of course, an enormous debt to many people for what is in this book, and for the inspiration we have had in the writing of it. To name them, however, would perhaps unfairly implicate them in the blame for it all! However, as Jesus is the author and perfecter of our faith, so we believe that any credit whatsoever that there is for this work must be due to him.

Accordingly, it is to him alone, Jesus Christ, that we dedicate this book.

Mime

1.   *What Is Mime?*

Mime is at a low ebb in public popularity at the moment. In the 1950s, Marcel Marceau introduced it to the mass audiences of the world. Today, though, television rarely features mime, except as done by clowns and comedians. Robotics and 'body-popping' look as if they might be mime but, since they involve nothing beyond wandering around rather mechanically, they are more forms of dance. Hypnotically watchable, but particularly devoid of human values and feelings.

Most people think of mime as a mysterious and exotic art form to be found (and best left) at the local avant-garde arts centre. Or else it is a kind of charades in the theatre, the principal entertainment being to try and guess what the mime artist is doing. If you are particularly quick then his antics might just raise a smile in recognition of some of the foibles and follies of mankind.

It was not always so. Mime has in some form or other been part of man's religious and dramatic expression ever since he was created. Primitive tribes still act out in pantomime the day's kill around the fire at night—an example of what might be called 'cultural mime'. Such mime is also a part of imitative dances, historical pageant and religious ritual of all kinds. Not least, of course, is the use of movement (kneeling, standing, raising arms) and symbolic action (breaking bread) in the Christian celebration of communion. The gesture goes beyond the words and, as a sacrament, it partakes of the spiritual reality it expresses.

As spectacle, mime has an ancient tradition, coinciding with the very beginnings of theatre itself. The Greek word *mimeomai,* to imitate, is a description of what theatre is about. In Greek and Roman times, mime was, as far as we can gather, a kind of mimodrama accompanied by narration, in which oral explanation and the actions of the mime artists were interwoven. Social comment and contemporary satire were often the themes. There were apparently solo mime artists who were celebrated for their special gifts of mimicry. They delighted audiences with their imitations of birds, animals and everyday sounds, or even giving the impression they were several individuals. Those were the Good Old, Old Old days.

Or were they? It was certainly no life for a young Christian. Tarred with the same brush of immorality as the theatre, and not without reason, mime was clearly banned by the early church. Yet from the tenth century the church, in response to the changing social scene, began to be the patron of religious drama. The mystery and morality plays, direct forerunners of our own English dramatic tradition, often incorporated or were performed in mime.

The sixteenth century saw the rise in Italy of a bawdy and secular theatre called *Commedia dell'Arte,* which soon spread throughout Europe. Highly farcical, it used acrobatics and juggling as well as limited dialogue. In its use of movement it was a virtual explosion of mime. Some of its stock characters, like Petronello, who developed into the mournful Pierrot, and the clown-like Harlequin, are still with us today. Harlequino used an actual 'slap-stick', for obvious purposes, and the term now describes pretty well what went on.

The resemblance with the silent mime theatre we know

today would still have been slight. It was a Bohemian acrobat named Jean Gaspard Deburau who, in the Parisian fairs in the first half of the nineteenth century, personally developed mime from crude slapstick to more controlled movement and greater subtlety of character. His Pierrot was immortalized by Jean Louis Barrault in the classic film *Les Enfants du Paradis*.

Three names stand out in recent mime history: Etienne Decroux, Barrault, and of course Marcel Marceau. Working together in Paris in the early 1930s, Decroux and Barrault began to develop the techniques and elements of movement isolations which any mime artist today must study and understand if he wishes to use his body to communicate. Decroux took this further than anyone and may truly be called the grandfather of mime.

Marcel Marceau was a pupil of Decroux, and virtually single-handedly (he used both, actually) popularized the art of mime in the second half of this century. His *pantomimes du style*, stylistic mimes showing how a man does things, are classic, and his everyman character Bip is loved by millions.

Marceau, now sixty, is less and less to be seen, and mime is ebbing out of the public's attention and appreciation. There is no one around to take his mantle and, by developing the art form, capture again the public imagination.

Nevertheless, there are today hundreds of mime artists and troupes where only a handful existed ten years ago. They are not much seen on television, but arts festivals and fringe theatres are full of appreciative audiences for them. Perhaps the tide is turning.

But what *is* mime?

It is very difficult to produce a working definition. It must be broad enough to cover examples throughout history as well as present-day trends, while not so vague as to include everything that moves with the body. I am

tempted to call mime 'the art of using the body to communicate in any meaningful way that isn't dance', but I would
like to do better than that.

For Claude Kipnis, author of *The Mime Book:*

> Mime is the art of imagining the world with others,
> . . . by moving and positioning the human body.

The English theatre director and mime artist Lindsey
Kemp has said:

> Mime is not only the art of movement, but the art of silence.

Jean Louis Barrault is still more poetic. It is:

> The language of the heart expressed in the gestures of the
> body.

Marceau has called it 'the very art of silence', although
there is a paradoxical emphasis in his remark:

> Mime is not a silent art. It is the art of touching people.

Another comment of his throws an interesting light:

> Film is the art of creating illusion through reality, while mime
> is the art of creating reality through illusion.

One thing that begins to emerge from these definitions is
the 'shared' quality of mime. A musician can make music
completely on his own, as can a singer. An actor has the
sound of his own voice, and wonderful words to declaim,
while a dancer can happily dance by herself.

The mime requires an audience. He depends on being
understood. He is only there if you give him the space and
your attention. This makes him very poor and very
vulnerable. He can be comic, but a sense of loneliness, of

sadness perhaps, is always there, under the surface.

Maybe this is why we identify with him a little, and why we generously follow him into the reality he materializes for us out of thin air.

Kay Hamblin, author of *Mime: A Playbook of Silent Fantasy*, says that 'the mime artist speaks a universal language based on shared experiences'. If this is true, then something else is happening besides an audience's merely being able to figure out what the mime artist is doing: 'Ah yes, he's unfolding the picnic blanket...how quaint.' A deeper communication takes place in a recognition that is *felt* as much as figured out. How many words about loneliness, sadness or depression does it take to evoke that feeling in the hearer? And yet when I turn aside my eyes, silently let my chest rise and fall, change the expression of my mouth ever so slightly, I find a certain fire goes out of my eyes as well. To *mime* this is to invite the audience into that feeling. They don't just say, 'Ah, he's depressed.' It is as if their body recognizes the movements—and so they can actually share in the moment. Well, do not take my word for it. Go to a mime performance, and see for yourself.

My own observation is that for the Christian performer, committed not only to entertainment but also to communicating himself as God has made—and remade—him, mime is a very special resource because of the bond it creates between him and the audience. The mime artist works with everyday gestures to create pure fantasy. On the other hand, he works with elaborate technique and skilled illusion to communicate solid reality—the reality of the human experience in virtually all its dimensions.

2. *Mime in the Church*

The heavens are telling the glory of God;
and the firmament proclaims his handiwork.
Day to day pours forth speech,
    and night to night declares knowledge.
There is no speech, nor are there words;
    their voice goes out through all the earth,
    and their words to the end of the world
                            (Ps 19:1–4, RSV)

A still small voice

Modern men and women spend so much time avoiding
silence. As if traffic and industrial noise were not enough,
we surround ourselves with other people, blaring radio
(or 'personal stereo') and the ever-present television.
Video recorders now ensure we can have our TV drug, no
matter what is being transmitted, at any time of the day or
night. It is all part of a flight from silence. Perhaps it is
because, in the silence, you are going to encounter yourself
and all the unresolved tensions and conflicts God wants to
heal and put right.

The lack of silence in modern life explains some of the
appeal of a mime performance. It is refreshing, relaxing,

and reflective. A welcome respite, and a moment of peace.

When the sound is removed, concentration on the visual increases. Gestures take on heightened significance, and a new language of the body is made possible, understood by all.

This should mean that mime would be welcomed with open arms into a church with forms of worship that embrace silence and meditative moments. There are no unexpected words, as with spoken drama, no noisy characters or intrusive personalities; and if it offends, you can always shut your eyes and pray.

But of course, it's not as easy as that—as anyone knows who has tried introducing something new into an established form of service, be it 'ancient' or 'modern'. There are a number of apparently reasonable objections to drama, apart from innate conservatism, and it is well to consider them carefully.

One sincere objection is that mime and other non-traditional art forms such as dance, banner-making, and modern music are basically *spectacle*. Spectacle draws attention to a performer, or an object of beauty, and away from God. It is therefore a form of idolatry.

This no doubt familiar argument harks back to the Reformation, but at base it reflects an ancient dualistic way of thinking—splitting life into the physical, which is bad, and the spiritual, which is good. God is spirit, it is rightly affirmed, and to worship him we must somehow mentally attune our spirits to his. Communion with God becomes a mystical or cerebral experience, without the rest of one's life being drawn in or affected. At worst, even our emotions and our will (i.e. our moral sense) can be seen as irrelevant. At best, body, mind and spirit are completely split up (and arranged in ascending order of value). How easily this decidedly unchristian way of thinking affects our religious attitudes!

Yet it is such an attitude that lies at the heart of the 'too fleshly' objection to non-traditional art forms in church or as part of our permissible 'Christian activities'. Drama—and mime in particular—appeals to the heart through the mind, by means of the body. Its raw material is people—people in all their 'createdness', both fallen and redeemed.

Let's by all means keep the world 'fleshly' to refer to sins and wrong desires associated with the body, which is its New Testament use. But do not use it to condemn every bodily activity. Our bodies may seem to inhibit our relationship with God at times—when they are subject to death and decay—but they are also the temple of the Holy Spirit, to be treated with respect and used to celebrate the fullness of life in Christ:

> Present your bodies as a living sacrifice, holy and acceptable to God, which is your spiritual worship (Rom 12:1, RSV).

Paul does not just mean, 'Keep yourselves pure'. As the chapter goes on to say, it is positive, wholehearted and, above all, loving actions that bring glory to God. This can surely include performances that build up the body of Christ.

Second-best?

There is at the moment a rekindling of the debate on whether or not rock music can be used in the service of the gospel. Part of the argument is whether something that is made basically for entertainment can convey a serious and spiritually life-changing message. Testimonies that God does in fact use music (and drama) to reach people are met with the objection that God may indeed bless activities that are still second-best in his will.

Stand-up comedians use speech—or oratory—strictly for entertainment, and some highly questionable entertainment at that. And yet preachers do not disdain the art form. In fact, it is part of their responsibility to keep the attention of their listeners, and to 'entertain' them in that sense. Almost all preachers tell jokes, or at least use humour. It shows they are human beings, apart from anything else, and often relieves tension so that they can really be heard.

As for the allegation 'second-best', the answer must be that we are not all preachers. We have different gifts, and those who are skilled in music, or drama, or dance, or banner-making, or cooking, or administration, use their gifts as best they can to testify to the God they know.

'But preaching—and administration—are gifts mentioned in the New Testament. Drama is not,' someone may say.

Neither are musical instruments, and yet we worship God freely using piano or organ. Christian radio broadcasts were inconceivable in the time of the book of Acts, and yet they are an important method of evangelism and bring hope to believers across the world. Stained glass is not mentioned. Yet for centuries, when there was no Bible in the common language, this art form was a primary communicator of Christian truth and biblical stories.

Why dramatize biblical material? The answer is in order to go out, in Wesley's words, 'into the highways and by-ways' of our culture. And with television as the dominant art form (or is it life form?) there is a need to communicate visually and dramatically in terms people understand—those people who watch television for an average of three hours a day, and receive virtually all their information in a dramatized, or at least highly dramatic, form.

Words, words, words. The church seems to be full of words, but lacking in actions that demonstrate the nature of God. One vicar, aware of the primary purpose of his preaching, placed a text inside his pulpit where he could see it as he mounted the steps: 'Sir, we want to see Jesus.'

Of course God *speaks* to us, using words—the Bible—and Jesus spoke and taught using words. He explained the significance of his actions using words. But God has also persistently and continually *demonstrated* his power and his nature—holy and loving, just and merciful. He demonstrated his promise to Abraham with the miracle of a son born to parents who were, by rights, past it. He demonstrated his power to Pharaoh with plagues. He demonstrated his care for Israel with manna in the wilderness, and his judgement of them with exile and dispersion. And his most perfect demonstration of himself was Jesus.

Jesus Christ was the Word of God made flesh. Sometimes it seems as if the church has spent 2,000 years trying to put him back into words.

What I am saying is that our services of worship, our liturgy, our corporate life need to be vital and vibrant, as well as reverential and meditative. Mimed drama, can be a vehicle towards the first aim while not offending the second concern. Always remembering that the Holy Spirit alone can sanctify our offering, make it pleasing to God, and apply it to people's hearts.

Silence that speaks

In a word-resistant society there is a particular value in mime that can 'talk' about things without using words. So often our words, especially our religious words, turn people off before they even start to listen.

Say the word 'judgement' and most people (Christian and non-Christian) think they know what you mean. It is a legal term, evoking God's reaction to the good and evil we have done in our lives. The *idea* of judgement, often accompanied by hell-fire images and a stereotype of gospel preaching, is very hard to circumvent in order to reach people's hearts with the impact of what God's judgement will mean.

Put aside then for a moment the actual word 'judgement'. Imagine, instead, several episodes from an ordinary life, depicted in mime with a few quick brush-strokes, as it were, and perhaps a shading of humour:

> . . . a baby cries, sucks his thumb
> . . . the boy plays football and fights
> . . . the young man makes a play for a girl
> . . . the husband does his best with a bawling infant
> . . . the worker trudges through his job
> . . . the old man regales grandchildren with
> a tale of war-time heroism.

But there is one more episode. This is after death. Change the lighting and our character is in a different world altogether. He looks around in wonder. Suddenly he is summoned. He must give an account. He rehearses the episodes, before the presence of God, in capsule form. Nothing particularly bad; but nothing, it seems, is enough. He finishes with a helpless shrug, and must leave the presence of God. He 'walks' away. Lights fade to black.

Non-Christians will often disagree with the idea of a judgemental God. But, when the word is not used, who can deny the logic and rightness of the *accountability* portrayed in this mime? It is an appeal to the heart and to the will. Before the majestic throne of God (imagined in this style), of what value are a few good works and a 'clean nose'?

That is not of course the whole story. The mime cannot tell it all. It is for the preacher to explain that Christ's death alone can make a life like that acceptable to God.

Actions speak louder...

Mime must be simple. Its limitation is its strength.
Gestures and actions that pass virtually unnoticed in the
course of a play or indeed in real life are chosen and used
for specific acts of communication.

In one of his silent films, Charlie Chaplin is playing a
wealthy playboy who is a bit of a lush. In one scene his
wife is fed up and leaves him, apparently for good. We see
him turn upstage to a table on which her picture is dis-
played. With his back to us, his shoulders start shaking,
and he seems to be sobbing with grief. However, when he
turns towards the audience, his face is perfectly composed
and his shoulders are going up and down not with crying
but with the action of mixing a drink in a cocktail shaker.

The effectiveness of mime lies in engaging the imagination of the audience. If they see what the mime artist
sees, and touch what he touches, then they may well feel
what he feels, taste what he tastes, and follow him into
any situation imaginable. It isn't just a communication of
so many ideas. It is participation in a shared act of
imagination. And the imagination can take us into the
most innocent and delightful play as well as the most
powerful and serious statements of life's truths with both
its tragedy and its ultimate hope of glory in Christ Jesus.

As you identify with the mime, you see yourself. If the
mime is vicious and cynical, you will see the worst in
yourself, and may feel condemned. If the mime is all
sweetness and light, and charming foibles, you will be just
as far away from the truth—(although a healthy dose of
good light entertainment is its own justification).

If, however, the mime artist has a measure of wisdom, if
he is inspired by the Spirit of God and has God's love in
his heart, then his prayer should be that people will see
themselves in his mime as God sees them.

See I have chosen Bezalel...and I have filled him with the Spirit of God, with skill, ability, and knowledge in all kinds of crafts—to make artistic designs for work in gold, silver and bronze, to cut and set stones, to work in wood, and to engage in all kinds of craftmanship (Exod 31:2–5, NIV).

Of course mime is not to everyone's taste, or even comprehension. Very few things are. Several times I have met married couples and been richly complimented by one half while the other frankly admitted that he or she hadn't been able to understand a thing. So much for mime as a universal means of communication. On the other hand, I may have given a bad performance that lost the audience through sloppy technique.

We are writing this book because we believe that mime can communicate the truth of God's message, his specific word or teaching to a particular individual or group at a particular time.

Here is an example of prophecy through mime and dramatic action.

Therefore, son of man, pack your belongings for exile and in the daytime, as they watch, set out and go from where you are to another place. Perhaps they will understand, though they are a rebellious house. During the daytime, while they watch, bring out your belongings packed for exile. Then in the evening, while they are watching, go out like those who go into exile. While they watch, dig through the wall and take your belongings out through it. Put them on your shoulder as they are watching and carry them out at dusk. Cover your face so that you cannot see the land, for I have made you a sign to the house of Israel (Ezek 12:3–5, NIV).

And Ezekiel did as he was commanded. He was a sign. 'As I have done,' he said, 'so shall it be done to them; they shall go into exile, into captivity.'

Similarly, Jeremiah heard God's word through watching

a potter (Jeremiah 18), and in chapter 19 he declares God's word through the dramatic action of smashing to the ground a potter's earthen flask 'so that it can never be mended'.

Are we so sure of our own understanding of how God speaks that we can put the story-telling and verbal arts such as drama, mime, songwriting and poetry into neat little boxes labelled *Entertainment: not to be taken seriously*?

Just playing around?

In chapter 41 of the book of Job, the Lord asks Job whether he is able, as the Lord is able, to play with Leviathan? But, we may well ask, of what relevance is playfulness in mime?

Kay Hamblin, author of *Mime: A Playbook of Silent Fantasy*, teaches mime on the west coast of America. Most of her students never come anywhere near professional performing. Instead they explore mime as *play*. This is an important aspect of the arts in general, which is far too often overlooked in the heated debate, learned criticism, and solemn 'enjoyment' that surrounds art today. Culture is the preserve of an elite who pride themselves on their sensitivity. Whether it is sensitivity to the subtle nuances of music, opera or the fine arts, or 'awareness' of the political overtones and social realism of contemporary theatre, the pride I think is the same.

The other side of culture today is equally deadening to the enjoyment and illumination that art should give. This is when it becomes another part of the 'new materialism' that seems to motivate the Western and Westernized populations. The motivation is to spend money to imbibe culture, in much the same way that the latest fitted kitchen just has to be acquired.

Where, in all this, is the innocent laughter? Where is

the joy, the play that should be part of the fullness of new life that Christ gives us? Such things are not childish; at least, if they are, they are nevertheless entitled to be part of adult life as well.

Jesus taught us that we must become as little children to enter the kingdom of heaven. Certainly his primary meaning was along the lines of an open acceptance of spiritual truth, as a child accepts gifts from his father. But we are over-spiritualizing and splitting body, mind and spirit if we confine such teaching to the mind alone.

Do we think that, because Paul writes in Ephesians 5:4, 'Let there be no silly talk, no levity' (which is translated 'coarse joking' in the New International Version), humour and laughter have no place in our lives? Our church services with their dull hymn singing and boring preaching, and often the divisive and almost legalistic concern for doctrinal truth, not to mention our attitudes to art and leisure, seem to be saying just that.

I am not suggesting that morning and evening worship contain a five-minute comedy slot to jolly along the proceedings. It is the rest of the week I am worried about. The usual response to a call for holiness 'seven whole days not one in seven' is to spread a dour and damp blanket over all our activities and personalities. It should not be so! However, I am mainly speaking of something special that can happen between a solo mime and his audience. A bond is created as they share a moment together. In fact, they are playing a game, with no competition, no losers, and very few rules. Equipment needed? A love for your brothers and sisters, the ability to laugh and the maturity to look at your own faults without feeling condemned and the faults of others without condemning them.[1]

[1]For a fuller discussion of the connection between Christian joy and humour, see the chapter 'God and Humour' in *Time to Act* by Paul Burbridge and Murray Watts. You may also be interested in their essay on satire in *Lightning Sketches*.

Perhaps now you will not misunderstand me when I say that we need to have more play in our church fellowships. This is to understand what the Fisherfolk call 'The Folk Arts'.[2]

Mime and dance—as well as music, singing and other arts and crafts—have a place in the church when we see ourselves as God's family. We are brothers and sisters before a loving Father who might just occasionally enjoy being with his children as they simply enjoy themselves.

Our hearts and minds need to be open to the whole spectrum of spiritual human activity that pleases God. This runs, I believe, from deep intercession and meditation, through acts of mercy and enthusiastic corporate worship, to folk dance and the ability to laugh at ourselves in a sketch.

In the church?

The use of mime in the church, after all I've said, should be limited only by the imagination, reverence and good sense of its members. The question must always be asked: what is appropriate to the situation? And we must remember, of course, that nothing these days is going to please everybody. This is why forgiveness and open, sharing relationships are so important in the church today.

Mime in church usually begins with the children. (We are happy to allow *them* to play.) By all means start with the children, if that is breaking new ground. But beware, it may reinforce irrevocably the idea that this sort of thing is *only* for children. If a greater freedom is there, mime can be seen in various roles in the church.

Mime in *worship* is most likely to be of a dance-drama type of presentation. Such performances use the power and vivid immediacy of mime and movement to reach people very directly. Sometimes the performers play

[2] *The Folk Arts in Renewal* by Martha Barker and Patricia Beals.

characters, and are as actors; other times they may work together to convey abstract ideas like the wind of the Spirit. Occasionally narration is used, and more often than not it is accompanied by music. Mime and movement such as this is often well within the capabilities of amateur drama groups. (Pure silent mime requires a much higher degree of technique so that communication is sure and unbroken.) Of particular value in this area is Gordon and Ronnie Lamont's *Move Yourselves*. Also, see the mime *The Valley of the Bones* at the end of my part of this book. Such mime is useful in worship for inspiring meditation and devotion.

Mime in a *teaching* or *evangelistic* role usually resembles the dramatic sketch, and as such may be seen as part of the preaching and teaching. Remember that television, whose language is drama, is the cultural equivalent to the public meeting places where the gospel was preached in New Testament times. If 'proclamation in the market place' is our ideal of evangelism, then drama must surely be a part of our preaching, though not a substitute for sermons. Mime in particular can serve as a visual aid or extended illustration. Usually, therefore, a point is being made, and we see characters or a character in some sort of conflict—the basis of all drama.

The particular values of mime in this respect are several. In a practical sense, where the acoustics of church buildings, as well as many street-theatre situations, can render actors' dialogue unintelligible, pure mime has obvious advantages. So does mime accompanied by one or more narrators using microphones or megaphones. The only question is: can it be understood? Is the mime clear? If so, then the audience, whoever they are, will have a much greater tolerance for semi-skilled mime than for bad or ham acting—the kind of acting that is recognizable a mile away by everyone except the actors and their mothers!

Also there is the unique power of mime and the art of gesture to communicate, engaging heart, mind and imagination. And if this kind of communication is happening, the mimes are speaking directly to their audience. They are revealing *themselves* with faults and failings, to be sure, and in all their humanity—but also as people whom the Lord has touched, redeemed and empowered with his Spirit.

This is sharing your faith. This is being a witness for Christ.

The use of mime, however, even as a tool for Christian communication, does not automatically convert people. It does not make a service 'modern' and relevant. In the end, it is always a sovereign work of God when his Spirit moves in the hearts of men and women. The final aim of mime in the church is simply to help open people up to that Spirit.

Mime is an art form which can, like any art, reflect the image of our Creator God, rich in beauty, majesty, grace and joy. As with drama, so mime deals with people and has the potential to reveal a God who is both merciful and just, and who, because he became man, understands our humanity. He has compassion for us, because he knows us.

3.   *Holding the Stage*

This chapter is for dancers. And mime artists. And actors, preachers, music directors and traffic policemen. Anyone, in fact, who has something to say and will have people's attention on him as he says it, and particularly if he is going to say it with his body.

The play *Children of a Lesser God* is about a deaf girl who falls in love with her speech therapist. I saw Elizabeth Quinn, who is a deaf actress, play this role in a recent production. Apparently she can speak quite well, but in the play she does not speak at all, while volumes pour forth from others who are 'normal'. And yet by the end of the first act, I could say I knew her character far, far better than any of the others.

They were all clearly defined types, and acted well enough. Elizabeth herself is not particularly striking to look at, but when she was on the stage, the whole audience was riveted by her every gesture. We had her sign language interpreted for us by others, but the words were never as eloquent as her actions. How many words does it take to convey the sense of a contemptuous flick of the head in response to a patronizing remark? Or the shock conveyed by the sudden look at another character, and then just the eyes following him around the room as he announces plans to leave?

I do not know what went on in the mind of that deaf actress throughout the scene, but it will certainly have been a mixture of thoughts and emotions. She may well have felt every ounce of the passion in her role at times, while at other moments she probably thought things like, 'That chair is in a different position tonight, I'll have to cross upstage on my final exit,' or 'This is a dead audience. No point in humorous sign language for a bunch of Japanese tourists.'

This is why it is so difficult to pin down the nature of acting in general and of stage presence in particular.

Concentration is one of the keys to what makes an audience concentrate. If you are involved in what you are doing this is unmistakable and involving in itself. That is one reason why televised sport succeeds so well: fine technique (and a close match) are made gripping by the obvious concentration of the players pitted against the clock or each other. All the while we are sharing in their concentration, and so in the drama of their match.

Of course, self-consciousness is the enemy, and concentration on technique should be done in rehearsal and be no longer necessary in performance. The actor is aware of himself and his surroundings, but the only thing that the audience should see is his absorption in the situation being danced, mimed or acted. For a mime this could mean an imaginary meal he is eating; for a dancer, a very real aspect of the Lord that he is celebrating.

Now this ability to be *absorbed* in the theatrical scene—dance, mime or drama—is not the same as concentrating with all your mind. It is not even always the result of such concentration. But I believe it is the other aspect of one's state of mind on stage that makes a performance watchable. So you must look for that gift of being drawn in, of fully participating in what you are doing. And it *is* a gift, it is part of your talent. And it can be very much a spiritual gift given by God to enable a performance to reach people, to touch their hearts, and sometimes to open them up to the Spirit of God.

How can I develop this gift, or bring it out of others?

A perfect example of concentrated attention and unselfconscious absorption is children at play. Can adults learn anything from children's games? Jesus taught us to be child*like* in certain ways, but surely playing games is a little child*ish*?

Clive Barker, in his *Theatre Games,* writes:

> Technical exercises tend to make the actor self-conscious...
> the [movement training] classes became a nightmare for me
> and we soon abandoned the exercises and started playing with
> warm-up games and improvisaton. We were working on
> extensions in space, and somehow just sticking our arms out
> didn't appeal to us. I suggested we marked a goal against a
> wall and that we threw tennis balls against it. The goal keeper
> had to stretch to catch the balls, not moving his feet away from
> the stance. The idea appealed, people enjoyed themselves,
> one actor at least was working...since then, I have never
> found a technical exercise for which I couldn't find a direct
> parallel in the world of children's game.

So when you begin the exercise sequence in 'Make It Work', stretching up with alternate arms, try *reaching* up with hunger and real desire for a succulent fruit—some grapes that are just beyond your grasp. Then see if your movement doesn't take on a new energy, and see if some of that crippling self-consciousness doesn't fade away.

If you are interested in dance or mime, then the technical exercises Clive Barker's students found so difficult will be less so for you. Which is just as well, because you *do* need to be in control of your body, down to the smallest facial expression and the smallest finger. This is the other side to holding the stage.

Eyes

Try this exercise in your group, from Richmond Shepard's

Mime: The Technique of Silence:

> One person sits in a chair, facing the rest of the group, and
> back about ten or fifteen feet. He is to use only his eyes, and is
> to communicate an idea, a story, or an event. He is to try not
> to use the rest of his face, and is to keep his body still. It might
> be watching a sporting event, or waiting for someone who
> either does or does not come, or seeing an insect, or a monster,
> or anything else.

Shepard remarks that as people both do this and watch
others, they may realize how much attention can be commanded with just the eyes. To use the eyes in an isolated
fashion on the stage can be quite dramatic.

Control different parts of your body in this way and you
have begun the training of a mime or of a dancer.

The mirror

Another exercise in isolation of movement is called *The
Mirror;* it also develops concentration. Find a partner of
roughly the same height and build and face her at a
distance of 4–5 feet. You are A. She is B. Now A should
begin very slowly to move a part of the body, say a hand.
Slowly, deliberately move this hand, as you did on the
floor in the beginning of the warm-up in 'Make It Work',
making different shapes and patterns of movement. Your
partner follows each movement of each part as closely as
she possibly can. The trick is to go slowly enough so that
her following is too close for an outsider to be able to tell
who is leading and who is following. Perhaps the movements are abstract, perhaps they are a detailed and precise
mime of making a salad, or brushing your teeth. But they
must be slow, to enable faithful mirror-following.

After a minute or so, someone calls 'change' and without
a break in their movement, A and B change roles. B
leads, and A follows. Change two or three more times.
Don't forget to try different parts of the body, and move

on different levels, not just standing. Let the caller vary the time between changes, so that sometimes a person has only a few seconds to take the lead, and sometimes she and her partner have a long time to develop the movement. Then let the caller gradually increase the frequency of the changes until the times are quite short, and the reflections are following freely and switching easily from leading to following.

Finally he should call, 'Both follow' and without a break A and B should both try to follow gestures and posture that are a continuation of the movements they have used up till now.

It is a real challenge and no doubt some will grind to a perplexed pause. When it works, it is rewarding and liberating. It is also a strongly peaceful movement when both are able to submit themselves to each other, neither dominating, but finding and going with the flow.

Machines

Perhaps you're not ready for that kind of concentrated attention on movement. If there are others like yourself, and you want something to get everyone working together, build a *machine*. Well, it's more of an automated assembly line really, made up of robot-like movements and mechanical noises produced by the parts themselves.

To start: one person finds a strong, simple action while standing, sitting or lying down which they can repeat endlessly without tiring too much. Invent a noise to go with it, and keep to this repetitive action plus noise at about one beat per second or whatever is comfortable. One by one, the group add on to this with different movements, and sounds to accompany them. First find the action—then add the noise. Have one person standing out, keeping time on a tambourine, or the back of a chair. When everyone is a part of the machine, he can play with the tempo. Slow the machine down to a crawl, or speed it up until it disintegrates.

For any age group, this is a fine and simple introduction to movement (and to each other). It is, moreover, worth repeating, to build better machines that have a wide range of actions, working on different levels and with a greater sense of both Heath Robinson and modern industrial efficiency. Pass on from simple movement to a conscious attempt to *be* a cog or lever or piston or spring.

This chapter is about holding the stage. *Machines* is the best exercise I know for introducing a group to the concentration and precision of movement which make all the difference between a shambles on stage which is boring and irritating to watch, and a group coherence that must be present in formation dancing, ensemble mime, or crowd scenes in a play.

Bus-stop

I've never forgotten the lesson taught by Edwina Dorman, my first illusionary mime teacher, when she took our mime class through this exercise.

Let everyone in the group find a simple action or 10–15 second sequence that they might do while waiting for a bus. This might be stepping out into the road to look for the bus, and back, then checking your change. It may be feeling for rain, opening an umbrella, then closing it. It may be lighting a cigarette, drawing on it, then stubbing it out. Make it precise, and brief, and be able to repeat it endlessly. It must be every time the same, down to the smallest part, facial expression included.

Now line up five or six of these mimes as if they were all at the same bus-stop. It is helpful to have agreed from which direction the bus is expected. Silently and simultaneously the actions are played out. On cue—for example, a discreet cough from the director—unknown to those watching, all but one of the mimes freeze. Notice how the focus of attention is immediately drawn to that one still moving.

Now try the reverse, perhaps with another group: after a minute or so, on cue, only one mime freezes. If the other mimes are really precise and repetitive, our attention is almost as strongly attracted by the one who suddenly stops moving.

Focus of attention is an aspect of basic stagecraft. But try the *Bus-stop* to remind yourself how important it is to know who is holding the stage, and how. And when you are alone on the stage, be aware of what part of you is the focus. Is it your face, your eyes, your mouth, your hands?

Don't just stand there, communicate! You can't help it. So you might as well control it.

One of the most worrying obstacles to holding the stage as an individual performer is stage-fright. Butterflies in the stomach is a familiar sensation to all who have performed. At best, you are taking nervous energy and converting it into a heightened awareness—mentally, physically and spiritually—of the situation. At its worst you are in the paralysing grip of fear, fear of failure, of making a fool of yourself, of forgetting where you are supposed to be or what you are supposed to say.

Famous actresses testify that they are always sick just before performances which nevertheless go brilliantly for them. This makes us think stage-fright is inevitable. It is not. Such a deeply paralysing reaction is fear, and it is lack of faith in a God who is God of the performing arts as much as every part of creation.

So now you get stage-fright *and* you are feeling guilty for your lack of faith. Don't let it happen. Instead:

1. *Examine your attitudes.* What am I afraid of? Do I need to get this nervous? Can't God use our mistakes? And do I think he enjoys humiliating his beloved children when they offer him something to the best of their ability?

2. *Purify your motives.* Is making people laugh (or cry, or turn to God, or even healing them) my way of gaining acceptance, of feeling loved? Do I enjoy showing off on stage because I am inhibited and insecure in real life? Do I open myself up on stage to an audience of many people to compensate for being unable to relate deeply to individuals? Do I covet the gift of dance or mime for the sake of acclaim, or even so that people will just *notice* me?

The need to be noticed is not sin. Children are neglected who do not receive attention from their parents. But if we do not appreciate and even bask in the attention our heavenly Father gives us, we *do* sin by transferring this need on a large scale to other people. 'Who can discern his errors? Forgive my hidden faults' (Ps 19:12, NIV).

3. *Trust your body.* Those who dance or mime can take comfort in the fact that when you learn your steps or dramatic moves properly, it is not entirely a conscious act. You do not have to remember a move in your thoughts before you can do it. Even when your brain threatens to seize up with panic, more often than not you can trust your body.

We never would have survived childhood if we had had to think about putting out our hands to break a fall. Performing is not quite as frightening as that, but it should produce enough adrenalin to see you through.

It is also a question of perspective. David Niven told the story of his first Broadway appearance. Although he had made many films, this was his first time on stage before a live audience, and he was petrified. A friend advised him, before the first night, to go to the top of the Empire State Building. He should look down at all the hundreds of lights spread before him. Then remember that his theatre was just one of them.

I have mimed before six people in a drawing-room and before 6,000 in the Royal Albert Hall. Both times it was frightening. My thoughts before going on were very much the same. My question was, would they be willing to share with me and able to join me in the conventions of mime I was using? Would they be distracted by the distance—too close in one instance, too far away in the other?

But the nervousness there hardly compares to the stage-fright I experience when I have to mime in church, especially my own. It isn't a fear of others' criticism. While not all may approve of this kind of drama in a service, there is never a whiff of criticism. And if there is, it is not for me to bear, but those who planned the service with me in it. And it isn't worry about sacrilege as far as the building is concerned. No, I think it is an acute awareness of the impossible-to-ignore stage quality of a white-face mime, contrasted with the atmosphere of corporate worship and sharing. What I do must come across as part of my own offering to the worship. Even more, it must be part of what everybody is sharing and receiving as we come before the Lord together.

You cannot please everybody, as any vicar or pastor will testify, but you should avoid offending most of the congregation if you can. Questions of taste do arise, and it is as well to pay attention to the feelings of others. Most of all, is what you are communicating part of what God wants to say?

But perhaps the greatest aid to putting a performer at his ease is the awareness that he and the congregation are one family, sharing laughter and seriousness together. They are at one when they rejoice before their heavenly Father in different ways, with singing, dancing and other artistic gifts.

Do you have a gift for mime? If so, it is given to you *for others*. Look to God to show you how to use the gift, and he will look after you and your gift.

Always his word is 'Do not be afraid.'

4. *Basic Mime*

In the chapters that follow I will be introducing you to the different techniques and approaches that are used in mime.

Again it is a taster and, I hope, an impetus to further study. To do this you will want to buy books on the subjects (see the bibliography), take mime classes wherever you find them, and above all spend time practising on your own and trying out on your friends what you discover.

Following each technique will be an example of how to apply it. For the sake of continuity, I am going to apply many techniques to the well-known story of the prodigal son found in Luke 15.

The prodigal son is so familiar to us that it is easy to miss altogether the points it is making. And the points all derive from relationships and reactions between real people. A son's foolishness, his father's generosity of spirit, a son's repentance, his father's rejoicing, and an older brother's jealousy. How, unless the story *lives*, are we to see the parallel with God's dealings with us?

There is not, in these pages, a fully scripted and blocked-out prodigal son sketch. Instead, I am using the story to give a framework for mime techniques that might be incorporated into a sketch as developed and presented by a hypothetical drama group. Costumes, number of characters, beginning and ending, are all still to be worked out. Perhaps there is narration or dialogue. Perhaps not. But keep in mind that mime should always go beyond the spoken word. It should not be merely actions that suit the words, but a dramatic representation that adds to the words.

Making visible the invisible, tangible the imaginary

To convince an audience of the reality of a world you are miming, you must believe in it too. This is the first step and it is a mental one. Concentrate on the object you are supposed to be using, or holding, or eating, or lifting, or whatever. What is its texture, its weight, its precise shape? Is it hot or cold to the touch, wet or dry? Even its colour and its past should be clear in your mind.

Don't just tug at the leash of any old dog, feel the leather around your wrist, and pull a small but tremendously strong Yorkshire terrier named Dennis who has other things in mind than going for a walk.

Related to this is your memory of real objects and actions. What do you do when you open a door, use a shovel, put on a coat, or have a coat or robes put on you by someone else?

Observe closely some of the things you do normally, and cultivate your memory of the feel and texture, the shape and temperature of all kinds of objects you handle frequently without thinking. Unless imaginary objects you handle exist and live for you, they cannot live in the minds of your audience.

The aim of the technique of handling imaginary objects is simply clarity. To achieve this, first learn to *separate your movements*. To begin with, take it to the extreme, so that the action of drinking is not just lifting your hand to your mouth and tilting it as you throw back your head. It is divided up: start with your hand down at your side. In front of you, let's say, is a full 'glass' of lemonade. Bend your elbow. Stop. Reach out with your hand. Stop. Open hand. Stop. Move hand to glass. Stop. Grasp glass. Stop. Bring to lips. Stop. Tilt up a fraction. Stop. Bring back to level. Stop. Bring glass away. Stop. Swallow. Stop. (Register relief, puzzlement, distaste?) Stop. Put glass down. Stop. Open hand. Stop. Take hand away. Stop. Return hand to side.

It is the kind of pause between each movement done so well by the robotic pair 'Man-Machine' you see on television on *Top of the Pops* and in adverts. The difference is that you want to remain human, so let go of all that tension in the rest of your body and take that glazed look off your face too!

In performance, the corners are rounded off, so to speak, the stops less pronounced, and everything flows more naturally. But there is always a hint of separate movements, which can only be conveyed by exaggerating at first, and then toning down.

This is of particular importance when you come to take hold of something. Approach an object with a completely *flat* and open hand. Always make a very pronounced 'snap' when you contact anything. It is that stop or 'snap' on contact that conveys the inanimate, concrete reality of the object. Then 'take' it in one motion.

Even more important is letting go. First *release* the object (make your hand flat again) stop, and only then *remove* your hand.

So the sequence is flat, stop, take—release, stop, remove. In this way, the viewer is absolutely clear that you are holding something or that you have left it behind. Keep your fingers together for anything smaller than a chest of drawers.

If you are holding something quite small, like a needle or cherry, just use thumb and forefinger. Curl the other fingers in, or splay them out, as you prefer. But still

approach with thumb and forefinger 'flat' and then take.
Release—and *then* remove your hand.

Clarity is also achieved through being *faithful to the
shape* you are handling. To practise this, imagine a pole, 3
feet long, suspended vertically in the air in front of you.
Remembering to separate all your actions, grasp it with
one hand, then the other.

Check the shape of your fingers. Is it a cylindrical shape
they are holding, or more conical? Are your hands directly
in line with one another?

Raise and lower the pole a few inches. Can you keep
your hands the same distance apart? Lock them, so to
speak, in relation to one another.

Now turn the pole through 90°, by rotating your lower
hand in place and bringing your upper hand down through
the arc. Stop. Release. Stop. And remove one hand,
replace it on the other side of the pole: flat, stop, take.
Likewise with the other hand. The most difficult movement is to bring the pole back to vertical, moving both
hands, still locked in relation to one another, and, by the
way, still holding a pole that is the same diameter top and
bottom. When you have managed that, it is a simple
matter to release, stop, remove the upper hand and bring
it down, flat, stop, take, and switch the other as well.
Practise often until your pole can be easily handled without
changing shape: lifting it, dropping it, pulling it towards
you, swinging it about, separating the movements with
tiny stops all the while.

Practise next with a ball, perhaps 10 inches in diameter,
which you seize and move about, rotating it smoothly.
Bring your hand flat against the surface, stop, and make
your hand into a shell, with your fingers defining a smooth
curve.

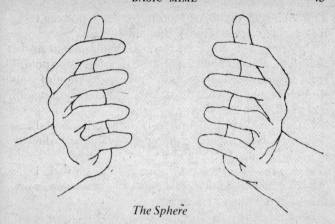

The Sphere

Making the shape of a cube is slightly different. Approach it with a relaxed but side open hand, and 'snap' your hand perfectly flat as you touch the cube. To release it, simply relax your hand in a single motion, stop, and then remove your hand, to replace it on another face of the cube. 'Take' all of the faces you can reach, twisting and turning the cube as you stay faithful to its shape.

Finally, clarity is achieved through *enlarging your actions*. Just make each movement bigger. How much bigger depends on the size of the audience. You will rarely need to make your objects larger in size, but your way of using it could be considerably altered if you have to project the action to the back of some of our larger churches, or a big theatre.

To achieve an 'enormous' action, communicating across vast distances, use the *wind-up*. This means you move briefly a very short distance in the opposite direction before moving a hand, arm or even the whole body.

For instance, you wish to replace a glass on a shelf at eye level. Before lifting it up, lower it by 2 inches and then put it up on to the shelf.

For the prodigal son, try picturing (in your mind) the

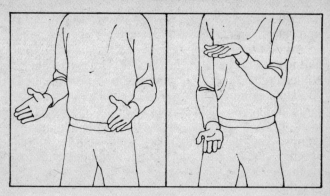

The Cube

two sons' inheritance as a giant biscuit, which the father takes from a big 'chest' in front of him. Holding it out, he lifts it high, and brings it down sharply on his knee, snapping it in two, and hands a half to each son.

Sounds crazy? Because this is mime, your audience will not only 'see' the slab, but will have no trouble accepting that it represents the son's inheritance.

But watch your technique! Finish off the shrug of the shoulders of the father, or the sad gaze at his son (if that is how you would have him react to his son's demand) *before* going to the 'chest'. Undo the two catches simultaneously with a single movement, then flat, stop, take the lid, and with a certain effort raise it up. Release. Reach in with one hand, grasp the slab firmly, thumb on top, fingers flat underneath.

Likewise with the other hand. As you lift it, give it (and feel) a weight that is *evident*, but still comfortable to handle. Show strength, not tension. Keep hands in line as you raise it up. Stop. Bring knee up. Stop. And break it in two over your knee, showing by the twist of the hands, now completely independent, that the two halves are separate.

Further on in the story, perhaps the prodigal drains his 'wine glass' with great gusto. Keep the shape of it as you hold it out (having just snapped your fingers imperiously for the waiter), let it drop briefly by a couple of inches as it is filled up, and now bring it more carefully to your lips. It is full to the brim. Freeze as the waiter hovers menacingly. Look at him. Watch his hand come out, demanding payment. Look front, then put the glass down, and pull out your wallet, which is empty, etc. Remember the focus of attention as it shifts from you to the waiter and back again.

If this scene continues, you may well be into a throwing-out-by-the-scruff-of-the-neck situation. When it comes to handling other actors, the convention in mime is that actual touch is avoided.

Always maintain a 'gap' and this requires really working together, whether the prodigal is kissing the hand of a loose woman, or being lifted out of his chair and thrown out of the door.

One tip, if you are going to try this. Say the waiter is to grab the prodigal's collar, haul him up out of his chair, propel him three steps towards the door, and boot him out. The prodigal, of course, cannot see the waiter's actions, so how is he to know when he is being lifted if they do not touch? The trick is for the prodigal to *lead*, and the waiter to follow. The prodigal lifts himself up, as if he were being pulled. He propels himself forward by exactly three steps. After an agreed pause—count 'one thousand-two thousand'—he flies off as if booted in the seat of the pants.

All the waiter does is follow the prodigal, while making it look as if he is leading. Simple. It just takes practice. But don't lose the power and conviction of the movement.

So you, the prodigal, must imagine that you are in a bear hug with a welcoming, overjoyed father who is half an inch larger all the way round than the actor you are hugging. And really enjoy that hug; put everything into it, and the audience may see more than two actors with their arms around each other, and more than a father's love for his son; they may even see the love of God for those who turn to him in penitence and faith.

5. *Character*

Now we come on to character in mime. 'Finding the character' is what acting schools the world over are trying to teach, and the process by which an actor assumes and expresses a stage character is a matter for endless debate—among actors, at any rate. Working in words and studying scripts, the actor can become very cerebral, with vast speculations being used to justify on stage the most extraordinary behaviour and speech. Individual gestures may be planned, but most of his movement is out of his control and quite unconnected with the character he thinks he is playing.

It is the same in real life. We spend so much time struggling to express ourselves in words that we forget how much of ourselves is reflected in our gestures, or lack of them, in our posture and in the way we move.

To take two small examples. In a group of people we will turn our head and use our eyes to follow each person as he speaks. But observe where your body is facing, especially your chest. Most of the time you will be facing the person who most interests or attracts you, whether or not they happen to be speaking. As Jean-Louis Barrault says, we look with the eyes, we see with the chest.

Another way in which we unconsciously express our-selves is in conversation with one other person. Whatever our relationship, but particularly if we do not know them well and wish to be positive towards them and to what they are saying, we will often adopt very similar postures to theirs. At the same time they may be doing the same thing, and you could easily go through a conversation having unconsciously adopted a whole series of identical poses.

The body speaks, often very directly and unmistakably. For this reason I believe that approaching characterization from the physical side can often be the key to unlocking the mystery of playing a theatrical role.

Start with observation. Make a point of watching people, in the street, in meetings, on buses and train platforms. Watch them as they wait, as they talk, and as they walk. Observe them on the news, and look at actors at work too, in films and on stage. Watch television with the sound down. You will begin by looking at the face and perhaps the eyes, but then try to look at the whole image the body gives, as well as particular ways in which individual limbs are used, the hands, the head, the feet, etc.

Doing this you may well pick up and store some mannerisms that can be deliberately incorporated in the creation of a stage character. The real point of such observation, however, goes deeper than that.

You may not think that such observation is possible for you to sustain, let alone usefully remember. In fact, our assessments of, and reactions to, body posture are happening all the time. By increasing, however slightly, our conscious attention, we develop our ability not only to imagine ourselves as this or that kind of person, but also to move in characteristic ways.

We next turn to specific activities in which we will eventually express different characters.

Occupations

Choose an occupation from the following list. (It's not for life!)

Bus conductor	Telephone engineer
Machine operator	Assembly-line packer
Teacher	Chef
Librarian	Secretary (no typing)
Managing director	Doorman
Gardener	Nurse

As in the bus-stop exercise (p.37), devise a simple sequence of actions lasting 20–30 seconds which you can repeat, smoothly and endlessly, and which typifies your occupation in the popular imagination. Make all your movements simple and intentional, whether of hands and feet, or face, mouth and eyes. Remember economy of movement, as well as separation, and handle all imaginary objects very precisely. Don't rush it, but prune out superfluous actions until you can fit the sequence into 20–30 seconds. Practise the sequence until you know it inside out, then show it others and have them guess the occupation.

Practise further with this one. Do the sequence in slow motion. Then do it very fast, trying not to lose clarity and precision. Repeat at normal speed, but very jerkily, with sharp stops and starts. Do it with exaggerated grace and flow, as if weightless, yet without slowing down.

As you become familiar with your sequence, begin to take it into yourself. Now *you* have that occupation, not just your body detached from you. And perform the sequence in different moods: dejectedly (fed-up and bored); breezily, cheerfully; absentmindedly; angrily; hesitantly (nervous). Create in your mind, if necessary, a reason behind your mood. Angrily grind out tickets and take money on a swaying bus, upset because you've just been told after two months on the job you've got the sack. Find the thought that will motivate you, and if one doesn't work, throw it out and find another.

How would you show a character who is a different age from your own? Don't be content with just bending over and hobbling a bit, one hand on a stick and the other holding your hip, and calling that 'old'. First of all think about the way different ages move. Here are some generalizations to help you. You will pick up others if you watch people closely.

In *infancy* there is an uncertainty about many movements. Arms and legs may be turned out, and often move as units. Late *childhood* is more abandoned, everything is limper and looser, with much twisting and turning when excited. Notice how the feet initiate many of the movements which then involve the whole body. Not so the *adolescent*—he often consciously restricts and inhibits his movements to avoid drawing attention to himself in the wrong way. It's not surprising he is awkward—he has lost the carefree quality of childhood, but does not as yet have the control of someone in his *twenties* who has begun to pull everything into place. (Instead of a slouch, with hips prominent, a more erect bearing takes its place, with the chest lifted as confidence is gained.) *Between twenty-five and forty* it is more difficult to specify, but differences can be found. The shoulders and lower neck are the first to stiffen. When a certain caution begins to affect movements, I think I can say we are into middle age.

In general the ageing process results in a gradual loss of flexibility, of speed, and of easy precision in what you are doing. Where once you would just turn your head to look at something, when a little older, it is the shoulders that must be turned, taking the head with them. Then the whole body, leading with the mid-section, is required, and at the end a simple look round may entail six or eight slow, shuffling steps.

Another way of grasping this is to think of a point in your body, below which there is movement, but above which things are beginning to seize up. Try walking as this point 'moves down' from the neck to the chest, then to the hips, and finally the knees for really feeble 'old age'.

What age is your character in this job? Be specific: a twenty-year-old bus conductor, a forty-two-year-old teacher, a fifty-nine-year-old assembly-line packer looking forward to (or dreading) retirement.

Think about the age you are supposed to be, and let your mind dwell also on images you have of other characters or people you know who are, were (or seemed to be) that age. Imitate the posture, mimic the ways of moving, act with the same speed and flexibility as you mime a specific occupation. Learn to trust your body to 'act your age'.

Thinking of character in terms of types can easily produce caricatures that are the stock-in-trade of a one-dimensional actor. They are like clichés that he trots out to avoid having to do any real thinking about the complexities of character.

However, clichés are clichés because they are true, and so it is with stage caricatures. Often they contain an essential insight about a type of person which is the key to their character. Once this key is grasped, you need to be free to unlock the door and able to go in and explore all the personal details and idiosyncrasies that make him a unique individual.

Physically, this truth can be surprisingly simple. Roberta Nobleman, in her book *Mime and Masks*, wrote this: 'With many stock characters, the walk, the body movement is governed by their personality, by the part of the body that matters most to them.'

This is something that can only really be appreciated or apprehended internally, when you actually try it. It is particularly evident when you allow a part of the body to lead when *walking* or *turning*. It is as if the part in question is the first to respond to a stimulus to turn or move, and the rest of the body follows.

The following examples are taken from *Mime and Masks*.

To play a **fat person**, you don't have to arch your back, and stick your stomach way out. Instead, *relax back* on your heels, and concentrate on letting the *stomach* direct all your movements. As you turn to face someone who has just said 'chocolate', it is your stomach that turns first.

Look at a well-padded Santa Claus, Ollie of Laurel and Hardy, Cyril Smith or Harry Secombe (as he used to be!).

Walking from the *head* shows us of course the **intellectual**, the clever, or the learned academic. The head leads the absent-minded professor and Sherlock Holmes, John Gielgud in many roles, but also Jack Lemmon and of course Groucho Marx!

The **tough** is John Wayne, Charles Bronson, Sylvester (Rocky) Stallone and Clint Eastwood. The tough moves with his *shoulders*, where all his strength is. Always ready for a fight, he feels his shoulders and they direct his movements.

Charlie Chaplin is our most famous **underdog**, but you will see the same body attitude in Woody Allen, Stan Laurel, or a sad clown. The walk of the underdog is in his *heels* and even if it is not always the exaggerated rocking walk of Chaplin, nevertheless the shuffle with the heels transmits itself to the rest of his body. *Down at heel* describes the character, and that is where his personality seems to lie.

You will find the **proud** looking down his *nose* at the world and everyone in it. It is therefore quite literally their noses that lead when they turn or lean forward to look at something. Charles de Gaulle, George C. Scott in *Patton*, world leaders and Conservative prime ministers have this bearing that seems to originate with the nose.

The **alluring** young and sexy type, male or female, will move from the *pelvis*. It is not just a case of swinging the hips, for it can be much more subtle than that. As before, the pelvis just seems to direct any action. Examples are obvious—Elvis Presley and female film and pop stars too numerous to mention.

The more innocent female character is the **heroine** or **ingénue.** Young or old, she is sweet, nice and unapproachable. She walks and turns with an emphasis on her toes, and sometimes seems to move with her fingertips leading, according to the time in which she lives. Roberta Nobleman's examples of classic *ingénue* heroines are Melanie from *Gone with the Wind*, Julie Andrews and Grace Kelly.

As I say, it will only be obvious if you try it, and it may not always work first time. But there is in these types an insight into character that can be perceived physically and emotionally, and can often be a startling revelation of the process of assuming a stage character.

With these thoughts in mind, let's go back to our 'occupations' sequences. You are in a position to build up a role—a person who has an occupation, and is of a certain age and temperament—all without speaking. Show others the sequence with age, character, and in an appropriate emotional state.

When you have done this, leave the sequence and find another, unrelated action, like brushing your hair and putting on a coat ready to go. Do these things as they would be done by someone of your occupation.

Finally, add motivation to the scene by imagining and filling in the details: where are you, who are you going to meet, and what do you feel like?

Now try some of the following occupations:

Farm manager	Farm labourer
Gambler	Bar girl
Pop star	groupie
Wine waiter	Animal feeder (speciality: pigs)

These are just a few suggestions that might be appropriate to a dramatization of the story of the prodigal son. Look at the parable and let your own imagination run to all the characters who might conceivably be involved in or behind this narrative. Slaves and masters, journeyman and gamblers, revellers and bailiffs, etc.

Build the characters up as we have done in this chapter. First convey the occupation, then a state of mind or mood, then age, then character type, and finally return to an action/mime that doesn't convey the occupation, but which is done as such a person might do it.

Apart from being good practice, bringing to life such characters often suggests details that can really make a sketch. Such details are the dramatic equivalent of the masterful story-telling techniques that made the teaching of Jesus so memorable to those who heard his parables.

6. *Illusions*

All theatre is illusion. It only works when there exists that implicit agreement between the playwright, the performers and the audience that they will pretend together for a couple of hours in a darkened auditorium. Of course in that pretence there is the opportunity to discover much about reality. As Paul Tournier, the Christian writer and theologian, said: 'Theatre relies on convention, artifice—the play is a "play" of personages. Yet one tragedy by Sophocles contains as much authentic truth about humanity as the most accurate biography.'

The illusions of the mime artist are more than that, however. In addition to the 'theatrical convention', he is conjuring up all sorts of images, objects, and places using just his body. But it is not the conjuring of a magician with his hidden sleight-of-hand and ingenious props. The mime artist performs his illusions for all to see. As Kay Hamblin put it, 'Mime is trickery by consensus.' The audience are not taken in, just taken along.

There is a moment, and it is a dangerous moment, when the audience say to themselves, 'How does he do *that*?' The more striking the illusion, the greater is the danger to the plot or story the mime artist is trying to tell. At best, however, the mime and his audience are stepping out of the convention to share a joke about the technique just being used to advance the plot.

It should be evident from these remarks that mime illusions should be used sparingly, and with care. Otherwise they are no more than party tricks with which you can amuse your friends. If that is all you want to do, fair enough. But remember that to the mime artist with something to say, they are always part of a larger theatrical purpose.

The famous *walk-without-changing-place* can be taught in a variety of ways. Usually a mime teacher stresses certain things in order to keep the walk in a particular style that he prefers. This version may well be subject to that failing, but really, once you have mastered one way of doing it, you should be able to vary its component parts and alter the style at will.

So we are going to learn it by breaking it down into parts. But first: to do this walk properly requires *strength* in the ankle, and in the calf, and it requires good *balance*. Have a look at 'Make It Work' and review exercises 12, 13 and 14. If you are determined to learn this walk in the shortest possible time, do them again and again day after day, and do them separately from the rest of the limbering. Then go on to do this one:

Lightly resting one hand for support on a barre or the back of a chair, stand straight, with all your weight on the inside leg. This we will call your supporting leg. Keep your other (the 'working' leg) straight, foot flat, but not quite touching the floor. Brush it forward and back once or twice, still with foot flat or 'flexed' and the whole leg rigid. Now: lift the heel, and at the same time, bend the knee of the supporting leg. Hold for a moment, then slowly lower the heel and straighten the knee. Repeat eight times on each side.

You should not bob up and down; the aim is to bend the knee as much as you can while staying at the same height. The heel lifts to compensate. The higher you can lift your heel, the better the walk will be.

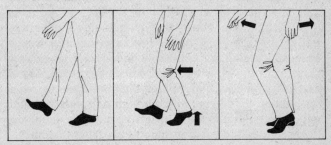

Fig. 1 'step'   Fig. 2 'pull'   Fig. 3 'start/finish'

Now the walk:

Use the support to begin with. Take your weight on the inside leg. Bend the knee of the working leg and, keeping the toes and ball of the foot on the floor, lift the heel. This is your starting position. Now lift this foot, and in a small bicycling movement, place it in front of you as far as it will go, with your heel no more than one inch off the ground (Fig. 1). Keep the foot flexed. In fact, hold that whole leg absolutely straight and rigid, and the foot as well. Now bend the knee and lift the heel of the supporting leg (staying the same height) and as you do so, pull back the working leg, still rigid, into place beside the other (Figs.

2 and 3). Finally, transfer your weight on to the working leg.

This is one half of the walk. Practise its step, going back to the starting position again and again, before changing sides and doing the same thing the other way round.

Note: 1. The working leg must be drawn or pulled back into place as against a strong resistance, like dragging your heel through treacle.

2. That same foot should not slide on the floor, but should just skim it, making no sound.

3. Separate the movements to begin with, with a tiny stop between stepping out in front, and pulling the heel back. And another between transferring the weight and placing the heel.

The two parts to each half of this walk can be called the step and the pull. The step (Fig. 1) is easy—just try to make it the same each time. The pull (Fig. 2) is harder since you are simultaneously 'pulling' your supporting knee forward, and pulling your working leg back. Say to yourself with each movement: 'Step' and 'pull'. After pull, of course, you are in position to step with the other leg, placing the heel out in front, 1 inch above the floor, etc. Now leave the barre and put the two halves together.

The hands:

Swing the arms from the shoulders, with very little movement in the elbows. Swing one forward and the other back and stop, so that the hand in front is about 10 to 12 inches in front, and the hand behind is less, maybe 6 inches. As you swing them, say to yourself 'pull'. As you stop and freeze them, say 'step'. Practise the arms on their own.

To combine arms and legs:

If the left leg starts as the supporting leg, with the right knee bent, right heel off the ground, then the left arm should be in front, right arm behind. Keep the arms in place as you 'step' and change them as you 'pull'.

Notice the right arm coming forward along with the left knee, and the left arm forward with the right knee. Arms and legs are *in opposition*. This is how they always are in a normal walk—with a slight pause to stylize it which can be smoothed out at will when the walk is mastered. At first, however, *go slowly*, and get it right. The strange feeling of uncoordination will eventually disappear, your muscles will get stronger, and then you can bring it up to normal walking pace.

This walk only works in profile, that is, sideways on. This is because at the centre of the illusion is the straight leg moving backwards past the bent knee of the other leg. In a real walk this is reversed: it is the knee that moves and the straight leg remains on the spot. The effect from the side, however, is the same.

The profile walk would work well as the prodigal son leaves home. Like all mime illusions, it must be acted, so a sense of departure, of looking forward and pressing on, along with judicious waving and looking back, are all necessary to the illusion.

At the same time, the father and elder brother could try the opposite to the 'walk-without-changing-place': changing place without walking. You will have done this as a child, moving sideways with a heel-toe step, ankles together, then toes together (Figs. 4 and 5).

Isolate this movement from the rest of the body, which stays, as it were, standing still, perhaps waving goodbye, shaking a fist or whatever, as you disappear offstage. If two or three characters can do it simultaneously, holding hands to maintain the distance between them, or linking arms, or hands over shoulders, the effect would be complete.

Remember the *focus of attention* and wait for the

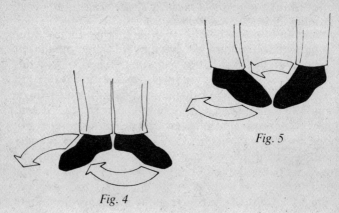

Fig. 5

Fig. 4

audience to take in the prodigal's walk before moving off yourselves. And don't be discouraged if you cannot master it in a day—or even a week!

Facing the audience, a mime has a number of ways to suggest walking, rocking from side to side, dipping shoulders, throwing feet out, behind, or to the side, etc. The following technique is, I think, the most effective with smaller audiences—say less than 500.

Use the back of a chair for balance, stand on one leg (A), knee bent a little, with the other leg (B) straight and slightly behind. The foot of 'B' is flexed, and lifted just off the floor. There is about 4–6 inches between the feet, and they are turned out slightly. On 'step', lift up the foot of 'B' and step on to the half-toe, knee bent, placing the foot exactly next to the other one. Straighten the other leg (A) as you 'step'. The legs are still turned out (Figure 6). Stop. On 'push', transfer all your weight on to the working foot 'B' (which makes you lean into it, but not too much), and slowly lower the heel, pushing it down as if you were squeezing your other foot out from under your heel and back. Do not straighten the leg of 'B' completely, but let your whole weight be lowered on to that heel. At the same time, let the 'supporting' leg (A) be 'squeezed' back 3 or 4 inches

(Figure 7). Keep it rigid and straight, foot flexed, as it leaves the floor. Stop. You are in position to take the 'step' of the other half of the walk. Finally, straighten the other leg (B) as you begin the next step (Figs. 8 and 9). So, 'step', 'push', 'step', 'push', etc.

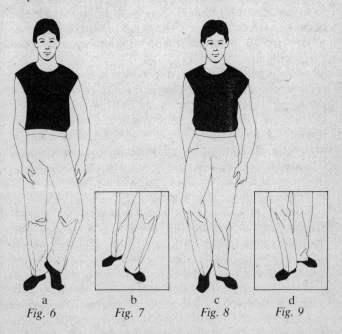

a	b	c	d
Fig. 6	*Fig. 7*	*Fig. 8*	*Fig. 9*

The arms work in opposition to the knee which is coming forward with the 'step'. So this time you have to swing the arms while saying 'step' and hold them during 'push'. Otherwise they are much the same as in the profile walk: one hand 10 inches in front and the other 5 inches in back although you may allow them to swing across in front of you by a few inches to magnify the illusion.

Once again, work slowly to begin with. Only go faster when you can do it smoothly in slow motion. And remember you are going somewhere, you are leaving somewhere else, and you pass people or things on the way. These must be real to you in your imagination, and they will be apparent at a subtle level in the way you walk.

The technique of *sitting* on an imaginary chair is useful to know, and very simple. It is included in this chapter because it is a stylization of sitting, and no attempt is made to conform to the actual shape we adopt when sitting—that would be impossible.

You will be well-enough understood if you simply bend your knees and 'sit' back about half as low as in a real sitting position. Go as far as you can while retaining your balance and keeping yourself more or less upright. It does not have to be very far down at all. The important thing is making a definite sitting movement, and coming to a definite 'stop' as you 'hit' the chair. Then rest your hands on the 'arms' of the chair, or fold them above your stomach, or open a newspaper.

You can even cross your legs, if you have the balance. Simply transfer your weight to one leg and swing the other up on to your knee.

When 'standing up', place your hands on the 'arms' and 'push' yourself out of the 'chair' by leaving the hands in place as the rest of you straightens up.

One last minor illusion: defining and moving along a *wall*. This is basically an extension of the precise handling of the cube in Chapter 4 above. The *stop* is all important here, as you 'throw' your hand from a relaxed shape into a perfectly flat position.

Only practice will enable you to throw the other hand easily into the same plane defined by the first, but this is what you must do. Check your thumbs, and for a wall directly in front of you, make sure they are the same distance away from you.

Pick up and replace each hand separately, for perfect clarity. Sometimes repeat the movement with the same hand, in slightly different places, as well as alternating hands to show the wall, or door, or box.

To *move along* a wall, place your hands on the 'wall' in front of you and slightly to one side in the direction you are going. Take a step in that direction, but concentrate very hard on leaving your hands where they are.

Or move along with your head and just the upper half of your body. To emphasize the movement *past* your parked hands, you can in fact move them 2 or 3 inches in the opposite direction as you shift your head and chest. Then let these parts surreptitiously 'relax' back to their original position, or even slightly to the other side, as you replace the hands—first one and then the other.

This exaggeration of the natural movement of one part of the body in relation to another is called *body echo*. Another example is defining a shelf above your head, or looking over a wall just taller than you are. Your hands stay perfectly flat and fixed in relationship to one another as you strain to see what is on the shelf, or over the wall. But as you rise on tiptoe—quite a small movement— emphasize it by bringing your hands down—as one—3 or 4 inches.

If you are meant to be actually pulling yourself up to see, let it show in the hands and arms, and don't forget to return your hands to their original height as you drop down again.

There are of course many other illusions, large and small. There are specific techniques to show bicycling, or running, or climbing stairs or a ladder. Space does not permit covering them here.

But wherever and however you learn them, remember that amusing friends and family is not their only use. Master the technique, and then offer it to your audience as part of a sketch that has something to say. And as you do this, remember to *act* it out, using your imagination to make the situation believable to yourself and thus to your audience.

You could, for example, use the second imaginary walk, facing the audience, for the return home of the prodigal. Perhaps you will make it a long and arduous journey home, with rock-faces to climb, streams to swim or fords to cross. Start out with this walk, full of enthusiasm following his repentance. As the journey progresses, you return to it each time with a noticeable flagging of energy. You are just about dropping when finally you catch sight of your father who has just come on to the other side of the stage (running towards you in slow motion), and the sight spurs you on to a last burst of energy (also in slow motion?) as you fall into his welcoming arms.

7. *Creating Your Own Work*

If you did not turn to this chapter straightaway, then you obviously have no problem finding dance or mime material to perform. Or you have an unusual amount of self-restraint!

If you *have* turned to this chapter first, you are in for a disappointment. There are no easy answers, only first steps on the way. Creativity is not taught in books. And if it was, we would not be the ones to teach it. Choreographing new dances and 'writing' new mimes are and always have been great adventures of faith for us.

Accordingly, all we can offer are a few comments and a very little advice that we hope you will find instructive. It is a short chapter.

The style and feel of a dance to be used in church and in worship must be absolutely right for the time, place and congregation. That is why no set pieces are offered in this book. The vast range of style of dance, and the way dance at this level is intimately related to the personality and physique of those dancing, means it would be wrong to suggest movements for you.

Where I cannot help you, however, God can! There is a simple direction for you to take, first steps you can make, that God by his Spirit will show. And *simplicity* is the key. If you have no experienced dancer to choreograph your group, this may be to your advantage. What you attempt will be simple and easily appreciated by those in the congregation who are as unused to watching dance as you are to doing it.

This isn't to say any old things will do.

If it is to be 'edifying' and upbuilding, the dance you do needs grace and beauty. Always strive for this. But remember that it comes from the inside, with the will to worship. That attitude can transform the simplest movement into a dance that is beautiful to God and inspiring to others.

As for mime, the situation is different, and the creative process is different. Again there is the importance of producing what is right for the situation, and you need to listen to God to find this out.

But drama is not worship. It is not and should not pretend to be God-centred in the same way as worship. The stuff of drama is people—with their problems, hopes, fears. It is comedy and it is tragedy.

One way of developing creativity is through *improvised situations*. Played out in the workshop with no more audience than the other half of the group, improvisation can reveal the bones of a drama sketch that is uniquely suited to the performers and to their church. Even the solo mime can improvise around a situation, although I find it easier if there is at least one person watching. For useful direction in improvisation, see Viola Spolin's *Improvisation Games*.

The usual advice when developing material through group improvisation is to have a director, however arbitrary and temporary the choice may be. Even if you are improvising mime by yourself, you could be helped by having someone watching who is sympathetic yet critical.

Don't get lost in the boredom and trivia of such stock situations as The Park, The Cocktail Party or The Bus Queue. Actors are always being given these titles, together with a few others, and then expected to produce something interesting and significant. It is no wonder 'improvisation' is a dirty word among even professionals.

On the other hand, avoid trying to create a sketch with the idea of expressing 'faith' or 'repentance' or some equally weighty Christian theme. Look instead for small pictures or parables like the ones Jesus told.

There were several aspects to his technique of teaching through parables that you could equally well aim for in a mime.

The first is that they contained memorable pictures, were easy to listen to and easy to remember. We don't know why the crowds heard Jesus gladly. Part of it was the teaching of the true good news, but when the teaching was in a way hidden from them (Mk 4:11), there must have been something else. He must have told a good story. The simplest mime, if it is done well enough to be comprehensible, can be entertaining in this way. Look to your technique.

Secondly, the parables often had a moral to them. Either they were an object lesson (the rich fool) or they embodied a piece of folk wisdom or a pithy observance of life's way (the sower and the seed). This made the story relevant to everyone, and not merely interesting.

Beyond this 'moral', however, was the spiritual teaching about the kingdom of heaven, and God's dealings with man. What you are looking for is a little story that succeeds on the first two levels, yet also expresses on a third level something about the spiritual 'laws'.

Do not try to draw out the moral and labour the point. That is God's theatre. It should be clear, but equally it should respect the audience's intelligence.

Do not try to spell out the spiritual meaning either. This is for the preacher to do. Whether people receive the meaning is dependent not on their intelligence, but on their openness to what God has to say.

You will only know a piece is 'successful' on this level by the uses God makes of it. If those who are hungry are being fed, then God is at work. If the deeper meaning is veiled for some who see the work and who appreciate the story, then it could just be that God is not speaking to them on that point at that time.

To create a piece from nothing, through improvisation or just mentally, take a subject like The Lost Coin, or The Smallest Seed. When you have a piece, give it a title like, 'The kingdom of heaven is like...' and see if it speaks.

One piece I do is called 'The good news is like...' In it a man is obviously fed up to the teeth with everything, but especially the ironing he has to do. Then he hears the phone ring, leaves the 'iron' (face down on a 'towel') and goes to answer it. From the change in him we see he is obviously receiving some fantastic news, like a pools win, or that his girlfriend is coming back. Even when he returns to his ironing, to discover a smoke-filled room (cough, cough) and a hole burnt clear through the 'towel', the news he's had has changed his whole attitude.

The mime described here is not original. I have to confess it was given to me as an exercise in a mime class in Paris. All I have done is create a character, added some humorous embellishments and of course the title. It then became a minor, but helpful modern-day parable.

Use narration. Then all the meaning does not hang on a single gesture that may be missed.

When working out the mime, don't suit the action to the word, go beyond the words. For example, the narration might read (as in Luke 15:14–15, NASB): 'a severe famine occurred in that country, and he began to be in need'.

How not to do it: prodigal clutches stomach on 'famine' and rushes around the stage, imploring the audience/other characters to have pity, etc., his face twisted in agony, with one hand outstretched, the other still clutching his stomach. Far too often he points, meaningfully, to his open mouth...

Instead, having been 'thrown out' of a restaurant for failing to pay his bill, prodigal picks himself up, and shakes his fist for a moment in anger. As the anger subsides, it leaves him waving his fist uselessly for a couple of seconds, before he lets both hands drop to his side with an air of despair. (Note the whole body will sag a little here, beginning with a dropping of the shoulders, previously lifted in tension and anger.) He dusts himself off, straightens his coat. At least he still has that. He picks off a speck of dust. He looks left. Looks centre. Looks right. Looks centre again. He lifts shoulders and drops them in a silent sigh of despair.

At this point, have a character enter from one side and walk straight across in front of our prodigal, furiously and with great relish gnawing a 'bone' or eating a 'jam doughnut'. Prodigal strains forward with his head, which follows the food as it passes inches from his nose. Three times this happens, until prodigal stops one and offers his coat in exchange for his bit of food. When he's finished (licking his fingers) the same man beckons to him, shoves a 'basket' in his hands, and as the narrator continues, points out to him the 'pigs' that need feeding...

Finally, always be prepared to accept criticism, constructive or otherwise. Seek discerning critics who will tell you whether you are striking that important balance between entertainment in the best sense of the word, and serious communication. That is the balance to aim for. Don't despair when it eludes you; rejoice and give thanks to God when it appears.

Appendix: Notes on Performing Mime, and Two Pieces

Some performance points

What to wear is always a problem. There are no easy answers, but please note that a uniform of blue jeans and a T-shirt will be most unlikely to flatter everyone's figure. Stretch canvas trousers are available which look smart and yet give great ease of movement, so give thought to these.

If at all possible, concentrate some sort of stage or flood lights on the performing area.

Make sure you have sufficient space to perform in, and rehearse in it beforehand.

If you do not have a high stage, then avoid or alter movements in the piece where the action is on the ground level for any length of time. Ideally the audience should be able to see the whole performer, from head to toe. Remember the short fellow seated in the fourteenth row directly behind the lady with the hat.

If facial expression is important, consider wearing some eye make-up, darkening the eyebrows and slightly reddening the lips, especially for an audience or congregation who will be some distance away. You might even want to use white-face, if its impact will be to good effect.

(The easiest white-face to apply is in pancake form: you put it on with a moistened sponge. A little practice will show you how to put it on evenly. Cleanse face thoroughly, though, before applying. Then draw exagge ated eyebrows above your own with liquid eyeliner or black grease-paint and a small brush. Enlarge the natural line of the lips very slightly with red/crimson/lake grease-paint and, if you are a man, outline the red with a thin black line. Line the lower eyelids, extending the line in a flourish towards your temple, and put some mascara on the lashes. A small thick black line one-quarter of an inch down from each eye will evoke the pathos of the clown, but if you choose to put a vertical line above the eyes as well, you will be turning your mime face into that of a clown, and a mime is not really the same. But it's up to you, in the end...)

Finally, do not look for high praise afterwards. Try to find out instead whether people understood what you were trying to do. If they didn't, don't blame them, blame your technique. If they understood something totally different from your intention, you should be equally concerned with your technique. Aim for absolute clarity and simplicity, at all times. Try to have an awareness of every movement you make, and have a reason for it!

Performing permission

Permission to perform any play or sketch should always be obtained from the copyright holders. In the case of the pieces that follow, because of the small amount of material concerned, a nominal fee of £1 is payable for the performance of either or both of these two pieces. This fee covers any subsequent performances in an amateur context (paying or non-paying audiences) by the payee or his group. It does *not* confer the right to reproduce the text in any fashion, and acknowledgements should mention author, title, and publisher.

The fee, for which a receipt will be issued, may be sent

to Steps of Faith, St Cuthbert's Centre, Peasholme Green, York YO1 2PW. Please include a stamped self-addressed envelope, and make cheques payable to 'Steps of Faith'.

All cassette recording, radio, television, video and film rights are reserved. Thank you for observing with us professional etiquette in this manner.

A solo mime without props: *The Offering*

Character (or C) enters upstage and goes to stage right of centre (as facing audience). He is late, therefore he rushes in and breathes heavily (and silently!) once to compose himself. He pushes open a swing door and proceeds down the 'aisle', walking in place facing the audience. He stretches, and cranes his neck, looking for a place to sit. First left, then right. He looks back to the right, smiles and gives a little wave to someone he knows. He takes a step or two downstage, still looking.

C sees a place on his left, stops and edges his way past people in the pew, smiling to persons either side of him before finding and settling down in the seat. (Be careful not to move too far to the edge of the stage. Remain fairly central for the rest of the piece.)

He bends his knees and bows his head for a perfunctory prayer, stands and picks up a hymn book. He peers up at the hymn number board, looks at his neighbour's book and leafs through to find the page. Holding it in both hands, he then launches into singing, with gusto. He throws his head into each open-mouthed 'note'. He really enjoys it—for about four seconds.

Suddenly C stops, looks left, looks down, eyebrows and face saying 'ah, of course'. C digs deep into right-hand 'pocket' and, pulling out a handful of 'change', selects a large 'coin' with left hand, dropping it in the 'plate' with a nod and a quick smile.

Takes up book from where he left it, and resumes

singing with even more gusto, Adam's apple vibrating, chest swelling, eyes closing a bit as he gets into it—for about three seconds. Then he stops short, eyes pop open, looks left, looks down, looks front—slight perplexed pause, then a shrug: 'OK'. C reaches again into pocket, pulls out change, puts down hymn book, makes to select a coin, then thinks 'Why not? I'll put it all in.' Shoulders lift, hands spread out, palms up. Face lengthens as chin drops while mouth stays closed—try it, you'll see what I mean— and he drops it all in the plate. Resumes singing with even *more* gusto.

Again he is interrupted—a flash of irritation crosses his face. He looks left, looks down, looks up to left, looks to right and left again (anyone watching?) and tries to wave plate away, but covertly, down by his side with his left hand as he looks forward.

He freezes after three waves, looks slowly heavenwards, smiles sheepishly, and motions to 'plate' to 'wait a second'.

C puts down book, then reaches into back pocket. He pulls out 'bill fold/wallet', opens it with both hands, takes it in his right, reaches in with thumb and forefinger of the left. Removes 'a note', places in plate, and freezes with hand over plate as he glances heavenwards. He removes another note. Same thing—pause—then a third and fourth and in quick succession. He hesitates over the wallet, fingers wiggling for a brief instant before pulling out and donating a fifth note.

With a (silent) sigh of relief he is about to replace his wallet in his back pocket, but he only gets halfway before he pauses, looks front, slowly brings it back out, looks at it a second and then dumps it into the plate.

He pats himself on his own shoulder for an instant with a little smile before he looks up, his smile vanishing and he makes a gesture with both hands to say 'Not on', followed by a nod of his head to say 'Agreed'.

C proceeds in this way, speeding up, and varying his

facial reactions to the Lord's 'guidance'; and trying to return each time to the singing as he:
— takes out cheque book and pen and writes a cheque, with several obvious noughts;
— removes a ring from one forefinger, puts it in, then another, from the second finger, and then about four more in quick succession, capped by removing his watch (offer up left wrist, palm up, 'undo' watch with a little twist of the right hand, and drop left hand away as right hand holds 'watch' aloft) and dropping it in;
— unbuttons jacket, slips it off, and ceremoniously places it on the plate;
— registers surprise, then unbuttons shirt from top down, pulls out shirt tails, pulls it off, and dumps it on the plate;
— wraps arms around himself and shivers but smiles bravely.
He then:
— resignedly removes shoes;
— sarcastically goes to belt of trousers—stops—looks heavenwards, gestures 'not on' again and a nod of agreement.

C tries to start singing, thinking that is all, when it hits him: 'Aha'. He slowly closes book, puts it down, places hands together and dives into the plate. Blackout.

Group mime with narration: *The Valley of the Bones*

This piece is based of course on Ezekiel's vision (Ezek 37:1–14) of the power of God's Holy Spirit. It draws a parallel between the picture of bones coming to life and ordinary humdrum lives being given joy, colour and free movement to show the renewing effect of the Spirit today.

The mime is for a group of between six to twelve people, plus a narrator. Musical sound effects may also be used, as indicated, or see the cassette offer on page 103.

One person is required to step out of the group to represent Ezekiel. He or she should be especially controlled and clear in their mime. The rest of the group will at times be trying to match one another's moves exactly, and at other times using different moves to give the impression of great variety. The piece should last about four minutes.

The narrator must work closely with the group, learning to sense when to pause and when to start up again. He should not rush the actors by reading too fast, nor should he allow great pauses to slow the piece down. He must know when to let the mime speak for itself, and when to carry on the narration over the action.

Again, the action goes *beyond* the word, and usually follows it; often it starts at the same time in order that it may finish a second or two after the last word of the relevant phrase. Leave the audience with a visual image, rather than a word ringing in the silence with no movement to accompany it.

On the other hand, there are moments (such as the very end) when all movement has ceased, and the words use the tableau or the last action to achieve dramatic and spiritual intensity: 'I have done it,' says the Lord.

Section I

And the Lord God took me and set me down
in a city full of people. They covered the ground,
countless numbers of them, and they were very
worn
5 grey
and near to death.
And God questioned me,
'Man, can these people live again?'
'Only you know that, Lord God.'
10 And the people groaned,
'Our lives are wrung and dry

Our thread of life is all tied up,
And we don't know who's pulling the strings.
We do the things we've always done
15 and do them all again.
We don't know why we're doing them
but thinking hurts the brain.'

Section II
We are fed up
We are *bored*.
20 Life is getting very *irk*some.
Work is pointless, living stupid,
nothing different, always boring,
make a living
keep a smile up
25 don't look down now
(whoopsee... bom!)
What did I tell you?
Up we get and on we go.
Mustn't grumble
30 Life can't be as bad as all that
if we just keep moving somehow.
P'raps it will get better
'cos it couldn't get much worse.
Life is getting very lifeless
35 and tomorrow and tomorrow
cre-eeps in this petty pace
from day to day.
Today keeps on creeping keeps on
crawling keeps on creaking
40 creaks on keeping
creak crack
crock up
crack up
crik.

Section III

45 And the Lord God took me
and set me down in a valley
full of bones.
They covered the plain, countless
numbers of them, and they were very dry.
50 and God questioned me,
'Man, can these bones live again?'
'Only you know that, Lord God.'
Then the voice of God came to me
clear and strong,
55 'Speak to these bones,
call out to them in the name
of the Lord God,
O dry bones, hear the words
of God Himself.
60 Behold, says God,
I will breath into you
and you shall live.
I will clasp you with sinews
I will wrap you in flesh,
65 cover you with skin.
I will force breath between your lips
And you will live
And you will know that I am your God.'
As I spoke, there was a noise, and
70 a rattling of bones coming together.
I looked and sinews joined them
Flesh hid them
skin covered them
but there was no breath in them.
75 Then God summoned the Breath
from the four corners of the earth.
'Come from the four winds
O Breath,
and breathe,

80 breathe,
    breathe upon these dead that they may live.
    I will put the breath of my Spirit within you
    O my people
    and you shall live.
85 Then you will know that I the Lord
    have spoken.'
    'I have done it,' says the Lord.

Section I

Line	Cue	Action
Line	*Cue*	*Action*
0	'Blackout'	Actors enter, take up positions, some standing, some kneeling, all crouched with heads down and with limbs *akimbo*—splayed out in angular positions to make grotesque shapes.
1–9	N/A	No movement. Let the scene impress itself on the minds of the audience.
10	'people groaned'	A single rise and fall of the chest of each actor, in unison, as if sighing deeply.
11	'wrung and dry'	All look up, mouths dropping open, to the ceiling. Just a head movement, in unison. Think of great thirst, and an image of baby birds stretching for food.
12	'all tied up'	Jerk into puppet poses, eyes fixed in face, glassy and staring straight ahead, still a little grotesque. Bounce arms and head a bit as a puppet does when coming to rest. In unison.
1	'who's pulling'	Walk (as a puppet walks) into places, making a circle or semi-

		circle, all facing outwards from the centre. Only two or three will be facing the audience directly, perhaps.
14	'We do the things we've always done'	Grasp 'iron' in right hand, place left hand on 'board' and iron across to left, to right, to left, then the right, each time on the beat.
	(Rhythm: ONE and TWO and THREE and FOUR)	
15	'and do them all again'	Iron towards you and away from you twice, on the beat.
16	'We don't know why we're doing them'	Take far corners of 'tea towel' and fold towards you, and then near corners and fold away from you. Neat precise movements, all in unison.
17	'but thinking hurts the brain'	Pick up and place on pile to the left, all very mechanically. Take 'iron' as if to start again. Freeze at end of line. Hold for two seconds.

Section II

Line	Cue	Action
18–19	'We are fed up, we are bored'	Typing (in an illusory chair, if all can manage it. If not, forget it).
	(ONE and TWO and THREE and FOUR)	'Carriage return' on 'bored'.
20	'Life is getting very *irk*some'	Same typing, 'carriage return' on irksome.
21	'pointless'	Stop, look at what you've typed.
	'stupid'	Rip it out of 'typewriter'.
22	'different'	Screw it up.
	'boring'	Throw it away.
23	'make a living'	Type again, looking down.
24	'smile up'	Jerk head up, as you assume

		manic grin—a mask of a smile.
25	'down now'	Look at what you are typing.
26	'(whoopsee … bom!)'	Hands up, then fall on bottom from typing position.
27	'What did I tell you?'	Stay down, frozen in place where you fell.
28	'Up we get'	Struggle to feet.
	'go'	All turn to the left, reach up to grasp 'strap' in bus/underground. 'Bus' jerks everyone as it 'starts'.
29	'Mustn't grumble'	Everyone swaying (hands holding 'straps' do not move), and bouncing to show movement of bus.
31	'moving somehow'	On first syllable of 'moving', all freeze an instant, then in unison reach forward to grasp another strap and move forward to it, still swaying and bouncing. Continue this reach-step-bounce on every other beat until all have moved four places on.
33	'lifeless'	Begin to droop and sag. Movement 'degenerates' and/or becomes mechanical.
36–44	'cre-eeps' (Begin to vary pace from 4/4 rhythm to suit the slowing down/cracking up)	Circle is slowing down, breaking up, knees bend as circle gets lower and lower; movements become more jerky, less frequent, then very spasmodic, finally ceasing altogether with everyone in twisted positions as at beginning (but much lower down). Pause four seconds.

Section III

Line	Cue	Action
45–49	N/A	No movement. Tableau speaks for itself.
50	'And God'	'Prophet' rises and comes out of group with a turn, to finish downstage right facing front.
51	'Man, can these' (pause)	He freezes on 'man', listening hard—very slightly bent over, but fully alert, head slightly cocked to one side. Hands spread out a little, eyes front. Snaps head to look at bones, snaps head back.
52	'Only you know that'	He gives a shrug, begins to turn away and walk up stage: not defiantly, but humbly ('such matters are too great for me', etc.).
53	'to me'	Freezes suddenly, stopped in his tracks.
55–57	'Speak to these' (narration builds as well to climax:)	He slowly turns, gathering intensity, summoning up courage and strength. Left arm comes down and across in front of body, then slowly rises in front of face, higher and higher until:
58	'O dry bones'	He brings arm down sharply as if commanding someone to be still, but with almost a chopping motion, using hand like a blade. At the same time he snaps head to left to look at bones. Holds this position.
60–62	'Behold, says God' 'I will breathe'	Turns hand slowly palm up. Lifts head slowly heavenwards, then reaches up gradually with right hand—he is receiving

		something from God with one hand and transmitting it to the bones with the other.
63	'clasp'	Hands come together, one palm up, one down and fingers interlock.
64	'wrap you'	Left hand grasps right forearm and vice versa, then slide apart.
65	'cover you'	Arm movement ends with both hands palms down in a small smoothing-over movement.
66	'force'	Hands quickly up, level with shoulders, then begin to push something (breath) down and towards a point level with your stomach and just in front.
67	*'will live'*	On 'live' hands come from only 2 or 3 inches apart together into clap which immediately breaks out into hands upraised on diagonal in praise to God, head up.
68	'And you will know' (pause)	Hold previous position.
69	'As I spoke'	Bring head down, cock head as if to listen.
	'noise'	All tap fingers on floor, making sound of light rain, and/or several notes played below bridge on a guitar or violin.
70	'I looked'	Snap head left to look.
	'sinews joined them'	All begin to move, still a little angular. Jerkily, tentatively all make brief contacts one with another, putting, for example, an elbow to another's knee, a wrist to a shoulder, etc.; all low down. 'Music' continues.
72	'Flesh hid them'	Run hands over one another's

		heads, shoulders, arms, keeping a distance of about 4 inches and avoiding contact; come up a little.
73	'skin covered them'	Same movement, but each to his own forearms, one and then the other. Stand a little taller.
	(short pause)	Slow last movement down and come gradually to a halt—eyes staring,
74	'breath in them' (pause)	seeing nothing.
75	'Then God'	No movement. (Possible music starts here: acoustic guitar or piano. Let a musician improvise as seems right.)
	'the Breath'	All *sway* very slightly, almost imperceptibly, to the right, and back again, once. 'Prophet' joins in on edge of group.
76	'from the four corners'	Sway again, larger this time, and back again. Do not move individual limbs, but sway using ankles and knees to tilt as a unit.
77	'Come from'	Larger still, a double movement of a small sway overtaken by a big sway. (Music builds.)
79	'and breathe'	'Contract' or curl up very slightly and immediately expand, uncurling a little as you literally take a breath. Arms follow the movement, in and out.
80	'breathe'	Same thing, more violent in, more expansion out.
81	'breathe upon these dead'	Same thing, bigger still (music still building).
82-84	'put the breath'	Final contraction/release turn into slow arms raising up, *all*

finish together with

... shall *live'*   fingers spreading out, hands
                          'snapping' into place to cap the
                          movement. Music peaks, and
          (pause)   stops simultaneously.
85   (softly) 'Then you will   Hold position to end of piece.
     know...' etc.   Listen to the word of the Lord.
87   '"I have done it," says
     the Lord'

Make It Work

'It' being, of course, your body.

The crunch question in this section of the book is whether you glance through it, or whether you start doing the exercises—and keep on doing them! Admittedly, it is not easy to do them on your own. It would be best to join together with two or three others with the same interest. Even if you are equally experienced (or inexperienced), let one of you lead the exercises regularly, reading them to the others to begin with.

Don't be daunted by the number of exercises. At first, just do a sequence of the ones you take to first. And above all, don't be put off by the fact that movement choreography and exercises make terrible reading. It isn't surprising, is it? It *will* be difficult to imagine what an action is supposed to look like. The only way is to get up and, laying this book

flat, try out each exercise or technique, step by step, until your body has learnt it. Let's be honest, there are some things you cannot learn fully from a book. But you can make a start.

Imagine trying to play a complex and beautiful piece of music without any rehearsal. Worse, imagine trying to perform without having practised on your instrument, playing scales and arpeggios until you are fast and fluid. The instrument just wouldn't obey the commands coming from your brain, no matter how strongly or sincerely you felt the emotion behind them or heard in your head the notes you were trying to produce.

You are your body and your body is you. But your body is also your instrument to communicate in dance or mime. And as any sportsman will testify, it is not the mind that learns the different moves and actions, but the body. My spirit affects the way I play football, or dance, or mime, but without training the body, the highest soaring spirit is effectively bound in any physical expression.

The exercises in this chapter are not rehearsals, for they are not pieces to be performed. They are not even the corporal equivalent of scales. They are more like the time spent by any musician simply 'tuning up',—but somewhat longer.

Tuning up will not take you very far, and it is well beyond the scope of this book to give even elementary dance training. Such is not taught in books. This is a start, and perhaps a taster. For those who have never been to a dance, mime or movement class, it will be an introduction to what goes on.

Before the work-out begins, there is a

section on relaxation, limbering, and posture.

Posture is included because in order to move well it is important to stand well. If you can control the parts of your body to achieve good posture while standing still, then there is a hope of controlling yourself when you are moving. You have to learn to walk before you can run, and learn to stand before you can move.

More important than that, however, is the control of *what*, or should I say *who* you are expressing. Even as you stand still, you are saying something with your body and your face, about who you are, and how you feel. Personality cannot be erased, therefore it is necessary to find a way of expressing a neutral character as well. So in the early days, at least, look at this section on posture regularly.

As you work through the sequence, and as

you repeat it day by day, or week by week, you will become aware of your body—and I am not referring to the aches and pains! You will see and feel how to control and separate different parts, and you will learn to be aware of what each part is doing, and what is the overall shape or form. The static control of the mime can be quite different from the fluid control of the dancer, but it must be learnt, just the same, through concentrated training and repetition.

Speaking of aches and pains, it is not my intention that you should sustain serious injury while attempting these exercises, or the techniques in the section on mime. It is important to take it very slowly and to work without strain at first. It also helps to work regularly. Naturally, aches will arise in muscles that have not been exercised for some

time or muscles you didn't even know you had!

If any signs or symptoms of injury persist for longer than two days, then you should take expert advice. But if you allow your enthusiasm to be tempered by gentleness and a respect for the body God has given you, you should be all right.

Dress for warming up is pretty much up to you. Stretch jeans or tights are ideal, with leotards for women and T-shirts for men, but anything form-fitting, that allows easy, unrestricted movement is OK: jeans if they are not too tight, or a track suit if it's not too baggy, or shorts. On your feet, wear canvas dance shoes, jazz shoes or very old ballet pumps. Even socks are better than bare feet, which won't slide enough on most floors. Training shoes and plimsoles are too stiff.

The sole must be very flexible so that your foot can bend and your toes can feel the floor.

What is the proper speed for the exercises? Music can be of great help here, as well as making it more enjoyable. After all, 'tuning up' can be a pretty boring business. If you can find some music—disco is a good example—with an eight-beat rhythm, and about sixty beats per minute, almost any sequence of exercises can be created to go with the music. *Saturday Night Fever* is typical—it shouldn't be too demanding to listen to. Tracks from Cliff Richard's *Rock 'n Roll Juvenile* are excellent. Don't worry at first about making all sequences fit the music exactly—just use the beat to keep you going. Later you can put music tracks and exercises together.

There are lots of records in the shops for aerobics. Aerobics, for those of you who don't watch breakfast television, is a keep-fit routine set to music. It is, I think, part science and part fad. You can even buy records for Christian aerobic exercises. But see p.103 for an offer of a cassette of music specially composed to accompany these exercises.

How you start depends on the warmth and comfort of your surroundings. If you are in a draughty hall with cold tiles on the floor, you may want to start a little way into this routine, with something energetic like running on the spot. If I can, however, I always start quietly and gently, and with a prayer to dedicate the time, my body and the use of it to God.

Relaxation

Lie flat on your back, feet apart, and allow

them to fall open. Palms up, arms at a slight angle to your body. Now press your body into the floor, piece by piece. Press your arms, your head, your legs, your back. Push them each into the floor for a moment, and then relax. See how much of your body can touch the floor—especially your spine—just by relaxing.

Limbering

Begin to move each part separately. Start with one thumb, and wiggle it around and around. Bend it, straighten it. Make it undulate. Then your forefinger on that hand. Now all the fingers together: wriggle them about. Start bending your wrist, as you make as many different shapes as you can with that hand. Then move it all from the elbow, and

when you have done that for a few seconds, let the whole arm move freely and easily from the shoulder: sometimes smoothly, sometimes jerkily, making elegant gestures, making grotesque shapes, but *all the while keeping the rest of the body still*. Lay that arm flat, and repeat the process with the other fingers, hand, wrist and arm. Do the same with each leg, starting at the toes. Do the toes separately—if you can! When you pick up your whole leg, try to be just as expressive as you were with your arms.

Finally, roll the head gently from side to side, then pull the chin into your chest, before doing the opposite: arch your neck to look at the wall behind you.

Lift your head off the floor an inch, and put it down. Again lift it up, a little more, and again lower it down. Use the length of your neck as you lift this time, and begin to lift your shoulders next time, and a little bit more of the back each time you lift, until you are sitting up.

Bring your feet in, knees up, and still sitting, slump forward.

Now *unroll* your back on to the floor, starting at the base of your spine. Let each vertebra contact the floor separately, until your back is completely flat. Now roll forward, bringing the head up first, then the neck, feeling each vertebra leave the floor, and when you are sitting, unroll one last time. With your knees up, you should feel the whole length of your back resting on the floor.

Hold on to that as you slide your feet out to straighten your legs. Now imagine you are made of soft wax, melting into the floor. Spread *across* the floor as well, letting the

entire width of your back and shoulders rest on, and be supported by, the floor.

Try to remember this straightness of the spine when we come to posture. Remember also this experience of letting go, and spreading out.

Sit up, put the soles of your feet together and, holding your ankles, bounce your knees up and down at a medium tempo.

After 10 or 15 bounces, begin to press the knees towards the floor. Work a little! (Dancers will recognize this as loosening up your turn-out. I say grasp the *ankles* and not the toes as some dancers do. It is a bad habit to pull on the toes, as this strains the ankles and encourages a terrible curvature of the line of the foot.)

Still in this position, turn your head, neck, shoulders and finally the whole back as you gently twist the spine. Reach around with your hands, take hold of your waist, and pull round a little further. Try to maintain a straight back, lifting from inside as you turn.

Posture

The posture you adopt while standing is important to the way you will eventually move. You may need a friend and a mirror to help you, but you must get it right so start now.

Stand erect, weight equally on both feet, which are slightly turned out and 6 to 8 inches apart. Legs straight, but do not lock your knees.

Tuck your pelvis under, but not too far.

Open your chest and shoulders, then lift your chest without pulling your shoulders back.

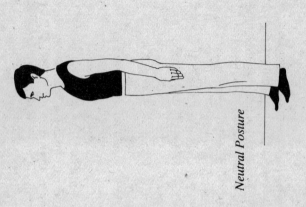

Neutral Posture

Think of a string pulling you up from the base of your spine, through your back, through your neck, the back of your head, and out the top of your head. Let it pull you erect, but drop your shoulders. Get your head level, letting it rest on the top of your spine. Keep your back straight, and try to recall the letting-go that was part of extending your back along the floor.

Finally think of your neck lengthening out of your back—the string again.

That's the outside. The inside of this neutral posture is equally important, to prepare you and your audience for movement to follow. Basically, you've got to 'keep the motor running'. You are not all tense and quivering; neither are you asleep and collapsed. The body is still, but not rigid. The face is immobile and expressionless without being frozen

into a mask. The eyes look to the middle distance, at nothing, but your whole bearing promises action. It is neutral—relaxed but alert—and it is a position you should be able to return to at any time.

Now, to begin the exercises, run in place for one minute. Faster. Knees up! Higher. Faster. Higher still. And stop.

The work-out

1   Swing one arm in a huge circle beside your body. Slowly at first, then faster and faster. Change directions. Do the same for each arm. *Don't dislocate your shoulders, if you can help it, but don't let the chest twist or turn. Try to swing just the arm in its socket in easy, wide circles.*

2 (a) Reach up with both hands, as high as you can. Stretch the whole length of your body. Reach with the top of your head too.

(b) Reach a little higher with one hand, then the other, 16 times. Stretch the length of each side of your body, from your toes to the tips of your fingers. *You can do this easily, or you can work at it. Let's work, right from the start.*

3 Feet apart by about the width of your shoulders. Reach up with your right hand and stretch over (and up) to the left. Bounce 7 times, to go a little further, and then come up on the 8th count. Do this 4 times to each side. *Stay facing forward with every part of your body, and don't collapse your*

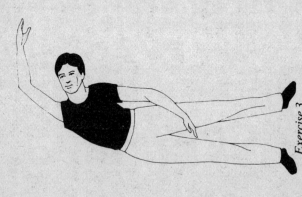

Exercise 3

*ribs to bend, but reach up and over
with your arm and your upper chest.*

4 (a) Now keep the feet in place (shoulders'
width apart) *and* the head and
shoulders over them, as you swing
your hips and waist in a big circle, 8
times one way, and 8 the other.

(b) Do it again, but much smaller, so it is
just the pelvis circling. Push it to the
side, tuck it under you, push to the
other side, and push it back. Change
directions, and do it 4 times. *This is
not a pretty movement, but it is important to be as flexible in this part of the
body as elsewhere.*

5 (a) Drop your head forward gently, until
your chin is resting on your chest,
then lift it up very slowly, beginning
at the base of the neck.

Let it drop to the back, and slowly
bring it upright. Now to the left, and
up. To the right, and up. Once more,
forward, back, left, right.

(b) Roll the head around, very slowly,
very gently, in one direction and then
the other. Twice each way.

(c) Look sharply to the left. Look to the
centre. To the right. Straight ahead.
Look up, look ahead, look down, and
look ahead. Do this 4 times. *Snap the
head into each position, and focus the
eyes at the same time on something
definite in each place.*

6 (a) Pull your shoulders forward, and pull
them back. Do this 4 times.

(b) Lift shoulders to your ears, and drop:
first right, then left, then both together. Right, left, both, and both again.

Do this 4 times.

(c) Finally, roll your shoulders, pulling them forward, up, back, down, 4 times one way, and then 4 times the other.

Many of us collect knots of tension in our neck and shoulders. This is a great treatment.

7 Put your arms straight out to each side. (Keep the shoulders down!) Now try to slide the rib cage across to one side, then back to the centre, and across to the other, 8 times to each side. *It is not a big movement, and the main thing is to keep the arms and shoulders parallel to the floor and perfectly straight as they move with the upper chest. The legs and hips stay rock steady.*

8 Rest one hand on the back of a chair,

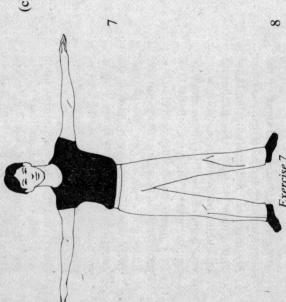

Exercise 7

or on a ballet barre, and stand on the leg nearest the barre. Brush the other leg forward, still touching the floor, and brush it back. Keep the leg straight, and point your toes in front and behind. Do it 16 times, and then begin to raise the toes off the floor very slightly each time. Then higher, and higher, and higher, until you are kicking as high as you can, in front and behind. Turn around and do the other leg. *All the time you are kicking, make sure the supporting leg stays straight, and that your back does not bend.*

9 Bring your feet together and put them at a 45° angle. Using the chair (or barre) for balance, brush one foot to the side as far as it will go without your pointed toes leaving the floor. Lower the heel and come down on that foot so your weight is equally distributed. In dance, this is called 2nd position (for the feet). Now do some *pliés*, or knee bends. Halfway down, quite slowly, and slowly up; then, all the way down, and up. Do 24 *pliés*, alternating half and full. *Keep your heels on the floor at all times, your back as straight as possible, and don't stick your bottom out as you go down! Do not hang on to the barre with a vice grip. Just touch it lightly for balance.*

10 Leave the barre, and lift the knee until the thigh is parallel to the ground. Circle your lower leg. Point your toes, and make 4 very precise circles in one

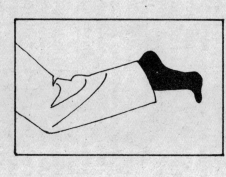

Exercise 12

direction, and 4 in the other. Change
legs, and do the other one.

11 (a) Straighten one leg in front, heel about
6 inches off the floor. Point the foot,
and then flex it, 8 times. Change feet
and repeat. *Again this can be easy, but
it should be hard work.*

   (b) Then circle it round, making small
circles with your big toe, 4 times one
direction, and 4 times the other.

12 Have your feet shoulders' width apart,
and put them at a 45° angle. Now lift
one heel as high as it will go, while you
bend the knee of that same leg. Do it 8
times to each foot. *Keep your toes on
the floor, as you force the instep out,
quite smartly. Make sure your knee
goes forward over the big toe, and not
out to the side.*

13 (a) Feet together at a 45° angle. Lift both
heels, keeping legs straight, to raise
yourself up, and then slowly lower

100

Exercise 14

yourself down. Do this 8 times.

(b) Do the same thing in 2nd position, 8 times.

14 Now raise yourself up, and keeping the heels lifted, bend both knees. Slowly lower the heels to the floor, and then straighten the legs. Reverse it: bend the knees, as in a half *plié*, raise the heels, straighten the legs, and lower the heels. Simple. Do it 4 times.

15 On your hands and knees. Lift and curve your back as high as you can, dropping your head and pulling in your pelvis. Now lift your head as you drop your back, pressing down for maximum curvature in the opposite direction. Contract and release in this way 8 times.

16 On your back for sit-ups. Do a reasonable number. Then do 5 more.

17 On your back, lift legs off the floor 8 inches. Open, and then cross one over

101

the other, open, cross the other way. 8 open, 8 cross. *Relax. If you're still with me, you've earned it!*

Exercise 15

Summary of exercises:
Relaxation—limbering—rolling and un-rolling spine—bounce knees—twist spine—neutral posture—run on the spot.

1 Swing the arms.
2 Stretch up x 16.
3 Stretch over x 16.

4 Swing hips and push pelvis.
5 Stretch neck, roll head, snap 'looks'.
6 Shoulders forward-back, lift and drop, roll around.
7 Chest parallel across to each side.
8 Brush feet, small kicks, high kicks.
9 *Pliés*, half and full, 12 each.
10 Circle leg from knee.
11 Feet—point and flex x 8, circle from ankle 4 each way.
12 Raise instep (bend knee) x 8.
13 Raise and lower slowly on toes, feet together, and in 2nd.
14 Combine raising heels with *pliés*.
15 Curve the back, up and down.
16 Sit-ups.
17 Scissors.

A music cassette by Chris Norton, with

102

voice-over to talk you through the sequence, is available to accompany this work-out. 'Music for Mime' features also the musical backing (plus narration, by Paul Burbridge) for two mimes, 'The Valley of the Bones' (as choreographed in this book) and 'Behold Your God', based on Isaiah 40. Price £3.99, including p & p. Order from: Steps of Faith, St Cuthbert's Centre, Peasholme Green, York Y01 2PW. Make cheques payable to 'Steps of Faith'.

Bibliography

Dance and movement

Doug Adams, *Congregational Dancing in Christian Worship* (The Sharing Company, Austin, Texas, 1971).
Doris Humphrey, *The Art of Making Dances* (Dance Books, London, 1959).
Gordon and Ronni Lamont, *Move Yourselves* (Bible Society, London, 1983).
Nell Challingsworth, *Liturgical Dance Movement* (Mowbray, Oxford, 1982).

Mime

(a) Technique
Kay Hamblin, *Mime: A Playbook of Silent Fantasy* (Lutterworth Press, Guildford, 1978).
Claude Kipnis, *The Mime Book* (Harper Colophon, London, 1974).
Roberta Nobleman, *Mime and Masks* (New Plays Books, Rowayton, Connecticut, 1979).
Adrian Pecknold, *Mime: The Step Beyond Words* (New Canada Publications, Toronto, 1982).
Richmond, Shepard, *Mime: The Technique of Silence* (Drama Book Publishers, New York, 1971).

Mark Stolzenberg, *Exploring Mime* (Oak Tree Press, Cowdon, 1979).

(b) Reading
Bari, Rolfe (ed.), *Mimes on Miming* (Millington, London, 1979).

Drama—general

Clive Barker, *Theatre Games* (Methuen, London, 1977).
Martha Keys Barker and Patricia Beal, *The Folk Arts in Renewal* (Celebration Services).
Paul Burbridge and Murray Watts, *Time to Act* (Hodder & Stoughton, London, 1979).
Paul Burbridge and Murray Watts, *Lightning Sketches* (Hodder & Stoughton, London, 1981).
Litz Pisk, *The Actor and his Body* (Harrap, London, 1975).
Spolin, Viola, *Improvisation Games* (Pitman Press, London).
Steve and Jane Stickley and Jim Belben, *Using the Bible in Drama* (Bible Society, London, 1980).

For further works on Christian dance, write to: The Sharing Company, P.O. Box 2224, Austin, Texas 78767, USA.